SECOND edition **REVISED PRINTING**

Marginalize THAT!

An Introduction to **MICROECONOMICS**

CARRIE Dibrell

and

Kendall Hunt
publishing company

Cover images © Shutterstock, Inc.

Kendall Hunt
publishing company

www.kendallhunt.com
Send all inquiries to:
4050 Westmark Drive
Dubuque, IA 52004-1840

Printed in the United States of America
10 9 8 7 6 5 4

CONTENTS

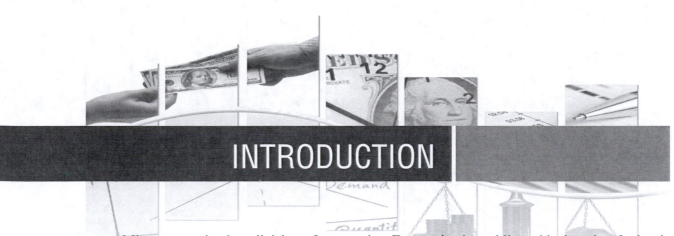

INTRODUCTION

Microeconomics is a division of economics. Economics is a philosophical study of what is best for people given the fundamental problem that everything is scarce. The older brother of Microeconomics is Macroeconomics. I call it the older brother because Microeconomics studies the building blocks that make up Macroeconomic issues.

I would like to share that I have been in the position of answering what economics is all about outside of the classroom. It is a hard question to answer because most people already have a preconceived notion of what economics studies is, and re-writing what people think can be difficult. As an example, when I am asked what I teach I am generally asked for investment advice. I am also commonly asked when I think the market is going to "turn-around." The only reason to make note of these various questions is to call your attention to the fact that the study of economics does not come with a crystal ball.

Rather, economics tries to answer what should be done about an issue that is problematic because everything is scarce. Economics is the study of scarcity. It is closer to philosophy and psychology than to accounting and finance. Economics is interested in weighing options against other options. Economists create templates and rubrics and theories but prediction is not a strong suit. The templates and theories are based on variables that are never constant. Because humans are the players that are doing the behaving, and because behavior is never constant, no one theory is a sure thing. So, the best answer of what economists study is that of options given that everything changes and is limited.

About the style of this book: This book is written with a specific goal in mind. I have provided only that which is *mostly* constant and left the remainder of the text *metaphorically* blank (because variables vary). As we go through the class, we will fill in the blanks with information that works. There is no **one** answer but some answers that are better than others. This in itself is how economics approaches most tasks.

WHAT WE WILL STUDY?

Microeconomics studies the building blocks of an economy. These building blocks will illuminate how firms can or cannot profit. With this endeavor, we will learn that there are some things a firm can do to *cause* profit but *much more importantly* we will learn about those things that a firm has almost no control over. By the end, students will recognize what factors are variable and what factors are fixed.

© Nataliiap.2010 Used under license from Shutterstock, Inc.

As it turns out, the leading theme in microeconomics is where profit exists for any firm, whether they have control or not. I will tell you now that profit exists where the firm produces at the level where marginal cost is equal to marginal revenue. It is possible that you will reject this equation because if revenue equals cost, then where is profit . . . ? It is completely understandable if this is your question: It is a good question and one which we will spend a lot of time explaining and answering. By the end of the course you will understand that microeconomic study is determining where $MC = MR$.

Before we begin however, I want to thank some people for helping me publish this book.

My first thanks goes to my children Robert and Allison. I thank you for simply smiling when you would ask "What are we doing today?" and I would tell you "I have to write," and that was ok.

My second thanks goes to Mr. McGinty: Without I would not have had the wherewithal, (starting with the laptop I wrote the whole book on) to complete this project.

My third thanks is to my mother. You are my inspiration! You set your mind to a goal and always accomplished it!

I would like to thank my sisters. I have three: Diane, Marcelle, and Renee. They are all far more intelligent than I am, and I invite them to chime in anytime they want.

Finally I would like to thank Janice and David: Without your loving support of me this book would not have been possible.

Economics | CHAPTER 1

So you want to learn about economics? Before we begin learning what economics is, it will be very helpful to extinguish any misconceptions of what economics is not.

Exercises are a key way to start any task and we will do them frequently throughout the book so we might as well start now.

Exercise 1

Think of four topics you believe economics studies (its ok to guess).

a. _____

b. _____

c. _____

d. _____

Good Job!

I am sure what you thought of can be connected in some way to an economic study. It is fairly common however for people to mistake economics for finance or accounting. In a random poll people said they believed economics is studied to teach people how to balance their check books, how to file their taxes correctly, learn how to make good investments, to know

what is going to happen in the future . . . sort of like forecasting people's behavior.

In some respect economics does investigate all of what people believe it studies but when

you get right down to it, economics is not studied specifically for any of the above.

When you look up the definition of economics you get answers such as:

ec·o·nom·ics n

1.   the study of the production, distribution, and consumption of goods and services (takes a

singular verb)

2.   the financial element of something (takes a plural verb)

Obviously if the dictionary says that economics is the study of production, distribution, and

consumption it must be right. It is all of that, but once you study economics you will see that

it is studied because:

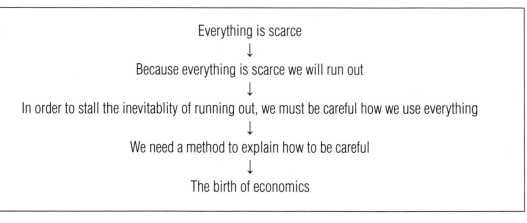

Economics Is the Study of Scarcity

> Let's use an economic tool to identify an ordinary problem!

Write down any problem you have today. (Hint: The bigger the problem the better.)

_____

_____

Next list the various reasons why your problem is problematic… in other words what makes your problem a problem?

1. _____   2. _____

3. _____   4. _____

5. _____   6. _____

Check through the various reasons you wrote down and see if you can find anything they have in common?

What do they all have in common? _____

Is the commonality of the reasons the same as your stated problem? _____

If yes, then you have identified the correct problem. If no, then the common ground your reasons share is your problem.

We will revisit this exercise when we start on economic systems.

Economic tool: Cost Identification: A problem is a problem because it carries costs.

Encarta® World English Dictionary © 1999 Microsoft Corporation. All rights reserved. Developed for Microsoft by Bloomsbury Publishing Plc.

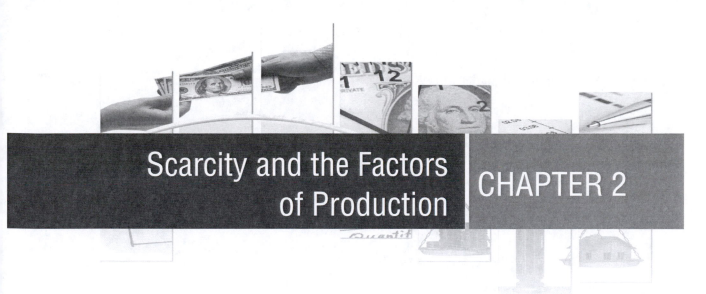

Scarcity and the Factors of Production | CHAPTER 2

Most people misunderstand what economics studies. It is common for people to think it deals with get-rich strategies, accounting methods, or even financial secrets to buying and selling stocks. Economic theories may attempt to reconcile some of these topics but none are the topics economics was developed to answer.

Economics deals with the problem of . . .

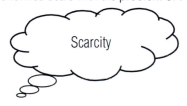

Scarcity

Economics was created to deal with a huge and unsolvable problem:

scar·ci·ty n

1. an insufficient supply of something

2. an infrequency of occurrence of something

So what does economics do with this problem of scarcity? Economics is not there to solve for scarcity but rather to come up with the best ways to use scarce resources so that their shelf life is prolonged. This means trying to find the "best" way to use resources that will eventually run out.

Economics is similar to psychology in that it studies subjects that cannot be fixed but still must be understood. Economics is used to uncover what the "best" way is, given that there is more than one way.

Since there is more than one way, several new questions arise.

1. What are the options?

2. How do we decide which is best?

3. For whom are the decisions the best?

Each of these questions deals with the idea of choice.

After choice is evaluated,

decisions are made.

It is because of scarcity that we must make choices.

Choices about what?

Choices about what is best, and

Best for whom?

The purpose of the economic study is to choose the best possible way to utilize (use) that which is scarce, and everything is scarce.

Scarcity

All resources are scarce. As a result, something always must be given up to get something else. This is the same thing as saying that there is always a cost. Economics is a study of the costs of what must be given up to get something else, and whether what is given up is worth it.

Economics Studies Scarcity

And

Everything is Scarce

↓   ↓   ↓

---

therefore _____

Think of something that you believe is not scarce.

_____

Why do you think it is limitless? (aka: not scarce)

_____

_____

Imagine listing everything that we know about in the world and checking to see if it was scarce or not. That would take a very long time (maybe doing that activity is never-ending). What if instead we developed categories where everything in the world is placed and then we evaluated each category. Economics defines five such categories and *everything* in this world fits into at least one.

Think of different factors (ie; things) that might fit into each category:

1. Land _____

2. Labor _____

3. Capital _____

4. Natural Resources _____

5. Entrepreneurship _____

Great!

We are talking about these factors because they are *"everything"* there is in the world and they are all scarce.

Let's have a discussion about these factors of production and show how they are scarce.

THE FACTORS OF PRODUCTION … (aka *everything*)

On the blanks below we will *defend* how each of the five factors of production are scarce.

- Land

Land, according to the Encarta English dictionary is

1. the solid part of the earth's surface not covered by a body of water

How do you defend that land is scarce?

_____

_____

- Labor

Even though not all people work, economics classifies people as labor with respect to a factor of production. This does not mean that population numbers are considered labor but more practically, the people we are concerned with are those capable of working because they can produce output.

How can you explain that labor is scarce?

_____

_____

- Capital

Anything that is man-made and is used to produce output is called capital. Capital is a factor of production once it produces real not potential output.

_____

Encarta® World English Dictionary © 1999 Microsoft Corporation. All rights reserved. Developed for Microsoft by Bloomsbury Publishing Plc.

How can you explain that capital is scarce?

_____

_____

■ <u>Natural Resources</u>

Anything other than land that is natural to the earth is considered a natural resource.

How can you explain that natural resources are scarce?

_____

_____

■ <u>Entrepreneurship</u>

The last factor is called Entrepreneurship.

An entrepreneur, according to Encarta means . . . "somebody who sets up and finances new commercial enterprises to make a profit."

How can you defend that entrepreneurship is scarce?

_____

_____

Recap → Economics studies scarcity ↓

Everything is scarce ↓

Therefore economics studies everything

So What?

. . . To enable _____.

Economics is a social science that aims to find the optimal allocation of scarce resources for the purpose of causing economic growth. Economics studies the various uses of these resources that will lead to their _____ (best) _____ (distribution). We need economics to perform this study because if the scarce resources are poorly or _____ employed, then the final output amount might be less than it could have been if the resources had been employed differently.

There are many consequences of misusing resources, some of which are:

1. We will run out of the resource

2. We will not grow

3. We might stagnate

4. We might die

Ok, so clearly it is important to not make sub-optimal decisions because poor decisions could result in economic failure, but what does economics help make decisions *about?*

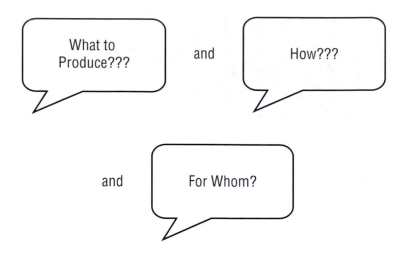

We are deciding what we should make with the factors of production; as in, what should the economy focus on producing? We are deciding how we are going to make this production (output); as in, should we use machines or people and from where? Finally, we are deciding who should we make this output (production) for; as in, the people with the money, or the people without the money or the domestic citizen or the foreigner, or for the government or for the investor?

Choice, Opportunity Cost, & Systems
CHAPTER 3

As we have said _____ is _____. Because everything is scarce we have to make choices. If everything were limitless we could have everything and we would never have to choose between anything. Unfortunately there is **nothing** that we can call a factor of production **that is not scarce.** Once we reconcile with the <u>fact</u> and the <u>constraint</u> that scarcity is unavoidable we realize that we have to choose.

I. CHOICE

How are choices made? This may sound like a very silly question, but in an economic examination, making choices is complex. Choosing is complex because no matter what choice is made, there is always a loss **and** a gain. Obviously, the desirable choice is the one that leaves you with more gain than loss. To figure out how to choose that which gives you more gain than loss, predictions must be made about all the various potential gains, set against all the various potential losses. This is an arduous task because it:

1. Requires predicting correctly

2. Requires including **all** potential gains and losses

3. Requires all variables that could alter either the gains or the losses stay constant (otherwise the information used to determine the benefits and costs will change)

II. OPPORTUNITY COST

Opportunity Cost is the economic terminology for picking between two options. It means that when a choice is made, another choice is given up (this is the loss).

Opportunity Cost is:

■   What you get (benefit), and

■   What you give up (cost . . . or the choice you give up to have the choice you choose)

Remember that because everything is scarce, choice is always there. Because choice is unavoidable, opportunity cost (_____ you _____ – _____ to _____ something _____), is also unavoidable. In regular language this is the same thing as saying that nothing is free.

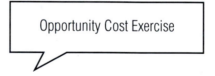

Opportunity Cost Exercise

Think of a choice you could make between two things: They could be activities, goals, food, anything!!

In the table below list the all of the benefits you can imagine about both choices (separately of course) and then list all of the costs of both choices (along side the benefits). Since it is difficult to assign a numerical value to see which choice offers the largest benefit in relation to its cost, at the bottom of the table simply count how many entries you have in each column.

In comparing the benefits against the cost of both choices, rational thinking dictates that you should choose the option that yields the **greatest benefit** in comparison to that choice's cost.

Choice _____   Choice _____

Benefits	Costs	Benefits	Costs

Total Benefit   Total Benefit   Total Benefit   Total Benefit

_____   _____   _____   _____

Next and very importantly, you must include the <u>benefits of the forgone choice</u> **with** the <u>cost of the option you choose.</u>

List below the total costs and benefits of the choice that yields the largest benefits against cost.

Choice _____ yields the largest benefits.

Choice _____ benefits are _____.

Choice _____ costs are _____.

The choice I am giving up is _____.

The benefits of the choice I am giving up total _____.

When I add the benefits of the choice I am <u>not</u> choosing to the costs of the choice I am choosing, my new cost is _____. In order to make a rational choice, I must add all of the inherent costs of the choice I am making with all of the benefits of the choice I am forgoing. The benefits of the choice I am making must still be larger than **all** of the costs for my choice, in order to maintain a rational decision. It is after both the inherent costs (direct costs) are added to the benefits of the forgone choice (indirect costs) that a **decision** is made.

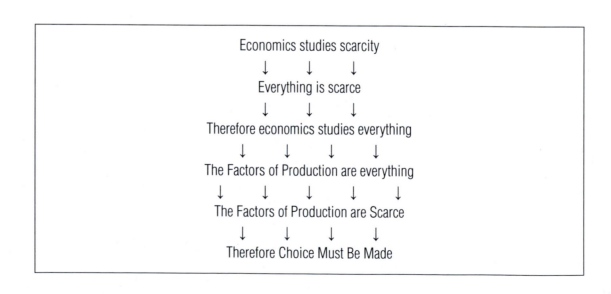

So what choices are there for economists to make?

Remember that the economic goal is _____. And also remember that all the resources we have available to produce _____ are _____. So the job of the economist is to figure out the best path to **growth** given that **all resources are scarce.**

What

The first question to answer is _what_ should be produced with these scarce resources?

The United States for example could specialize in the production of agriculture, electronics, the service sector, aerospace, medical equipment, or oil. There are many factors that contribute to deciding the opportunity cost of producing in any of these industries. Some opportunities include making use of those resources we have the most of, other opportunities include producing in those industries where we can make the most profit, and finally some opportunities include producing in those industries where no other economy dominates.

How

After answering "what" the economy should produce, the next question is _how_ to produce what is being produced. An industry can produce with people, natural resources, artificial resources/machines (capital), and entrepreneurship, and it can do so in a variety of combinations. One major concern is the cost of the factors used to produce. Another concern is how one factor can be combined with other factors. What else do you think might go into deciding _how_ to produce?

_____

_____

_____

_____

_____

For Whom

The final question to answer is traditionally described as "for whom" is the "what" produced? Upon first glance you might answer that the "what" is made for anyone that <u>wants it</u> and <u>can afford</u> to buy it. That is a partially correct answer but the full answer would say: The what is made for anyone who wants it and can afford it and those that can afford most of what is produced are also the owners of the resources used to produce the "what."

Most students are familiar with the first answer, (if I have money and want it, I *can* buy it). The second answer means that the "what" is produced for the people who are in charge of how the resource got produced in the first place because generally speaking they are wealthy because they own resources. Think big here. If you own the land that is used to grow the corn, then when the corn sells you will have the money. So while some may be able to consume the corn you grew, ultimately you own the land, the corn and the money. What might you do with your money? Perhaps you will buy a _____ that can be used to create _____ . And for your troubles in producing all of this output, you will have access to the output, and you will own the land, the _____ , and the money people gave you in exchange for what you produced.

What this means is; those that **own** the **resources** are "the whom." When you marry our two answers together, the full definition of the "for whom" is **anyone** with the **rights to purchase.**

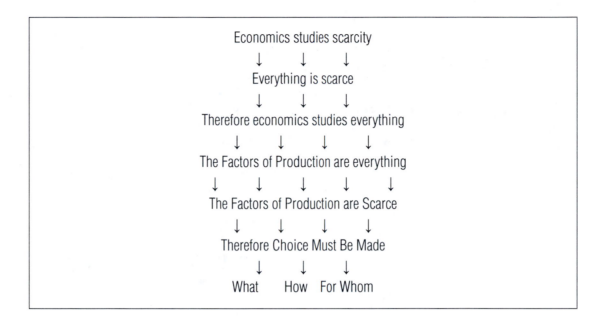

III.   ECONOMIC SYSTEMS

No matter what, all economies have the same three questions to answer: _____

to _____, how to produce, and _____ to _____.

Whenever questions are asked, they are generally asked for a reason. For example, when you ask for directions, your reason is to get to your destination. Or perhaps, you want to know how something works because you want to understand it. In both cases you have a goal.

In the case of economics we need to know what to produce, how to produce it, and who gets to buy it, so that growth can occur. Growth is the goal of all economics.

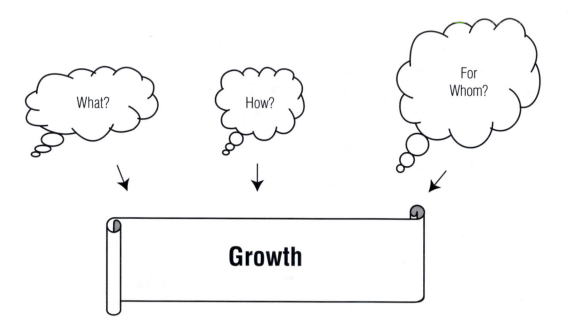

The questions on the previous page are all asked with the goal of "how do we grow?" In order to reach our goal, we need to construct a plan.

Creating a Method/Plan/System

When you ask for directions you probably spoke words . . . or used a language that would be understood as your method. When you want to know how something works you might take the thing apart to figure it out, and that is your method. So to reach our goal, (of _____) we need a method or a plan. **The method to reach a goal is defined as the system.**

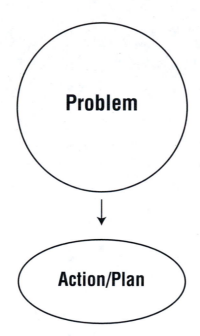

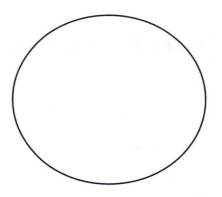

Exercise:

Think of a problem you
want to solve, but don't
know how. . .

In the above circle identify the problem you are trying to solve. Note: It is easier to solve if you narrow your problem down to one word.

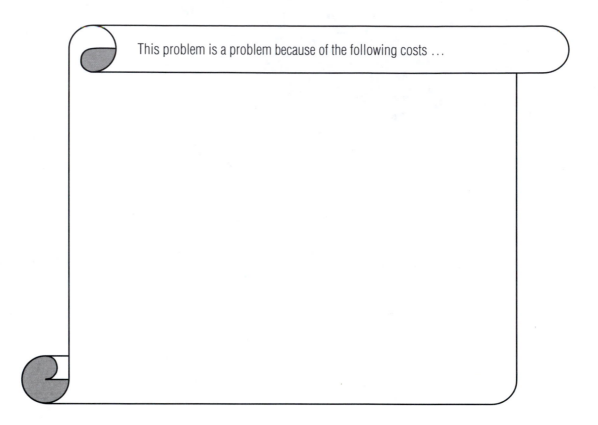

This problem is a problem because of the following costs …

Now that you have the problem identified, make a list of potential plans to solve it.

From the list above pick the solution/plan you will implement and write it in the middle of the bow.

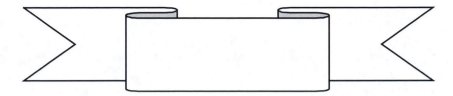

Next, write a plan of action that will implement your goal.

What you have created is a system to achieve a goal. In choosing a method, goals are achieved.

ECONOMIC SYSTEM OPTIONS

There are three economic systems to choose from: the Market, the Mix, and the Plan. While there are big differences between these systems, the main difference boils down to how freely price moves and decides the answers to what is produced, how it is produced, and for whom it is produced to reach the goal of growth.

1.   THE MARKET

The market uses supply and demand to determine the answers to what, how, and for whom. On the supply side are the producers and on the demand side are the various buyers. Provided with enough freedom to produce, producers (supply) will produce those goods and services that yield them the profit they want to earn. Similarly, given enough freedom, the buyer (demand) will purchase those goods and services that will yield them the most satisfaction (utility).

Where the supply and demand curves meet is where the decision between supply and demand is made. This intersection is called equilibrium and can be seen as the decision point regarding what gets produced, how many get produced, and at what price it sells for. Notice that all three questions are answered by this equilibrium.

- What gets produced? = What suppliers want to supply, alongside what buyers want to buy.

- How it gets produced? = How suppliers want to produce the good or service.

- For whom it is produced? = Who among the buyers is able and willing to purchase.

It is very important to note that where supply and demand meet establishes the answers to our three questions; and yet, the intersection between the two curves should not be confused with *the happy place.*

Shortage

Should suppliers be interested in supplying a good or service that many buyers want, the intersection between supply and demand (equilibrium) will be high up in terms of price (this intersection will be a reflection of strong demand) and possibly result in a shortage.

Surplus

Should suppliers be interested in supplying a good or a service that few buyers want, the intersection between supply and demand (equilibrium) will be low in terms of price (this intersection will be a reflection of weak demand) and possibly result in a surplus.

Price

Price functions as a communicator between _____ and _____. Price and quantity of what is produced is answered by where supply and demand meet. It is possible that those in supply and those in demand are satisfied with the price and the amount of what gets produced. However, it is also possible that only the suppliers are satisfied (shortage—resulting in a high price) or it is possible that only the buyers are satisfied (surplus—resulting in a low price).

Equilibrium

Ironically the word equilibrium ONLY describes where supply and demand meet. It does not mean that suppliers or buyers are equally happy. There is no conversation about who is better off where equilibrium exists, it simply is a statement of where the two curves meet.

- The market does not need a conversation.

- The market does not need to make things equal.

- The market functions by those who are willing and able to produce and purchase goods and services.

Where supply and demand meet answers

- What to produce

- How to produce

- For whom to produce

2. THE MIX

While the market uses the intersection between the supply and demand curves to determine what, how, and for whom; the supply curve is made up of private businesses and the demand curve is made up of various buyers, then it is really the private sector that makes all of the decisions in a market system.

The Mix economic system makes use of the private sector as in the market system, but it also uses the government in decisions relating to:

What to produce

How to produce

For whom to produce

The degree to when and how much the market is used over the government, is at best very vague. Generally where a social imbalance exists (with Supply or with Demand) the government may get involved. The terminology of **_mix_** works perfectly because there is no strict adherence to which side is rescued by the government.

Why Use Both?

The evolution of the system can shed light on what makes up the **mix** economic system. Under the Market system private enterprise is motivated by profit. Where an industry is profitable, suppliers are motivated to supply. Furthermore, where there is competition, buyers are generally not abused by the power of the suppliers, in terms of availability, price, and quality. When competition erodes (suppliers have all of the power) or where an industry is not profitable (buyers cannot access the goods and services they demand), the market system may fail to provide the best answers to our three questions of: _____ to _____, how _____ _____, and for _____ to _____. Under either condition, the government may step in to rescue the failing side.

When an industry ceases to exist because there is <u>no profit</u> or when buyers are abused by suppliers having too much power, the government can be used to:

- Produce that which is not profitable

  or

- Regulate where the buyer needs "back-up"

Typical Characteristics of the Mix economic system include:

On the Supply Side

- Subsidies or price floors (minimum price) for industries that receive government assistance or they will disappear (farming, education)

- Regulatory arrangements for industries that only generate profit for one supplier (called natural monopolies : utilities, public transportation, water)

On the Demand Side

- Price ceilings (where the price charged by suppliers may not exceed a certain level)

- Regulations relating to safety (FDA, OSHA, minimum wage)

- Regulations relating to safety-nets (social security, unemployment insurance, welfare, food stamps, subsidized housing, Medicare)

In general, the government is used to balance the needs of suppliers and buyers to create more harmony where co-existence between the two results in a socially undesirable location. Essentially this means that where the profit of either supply or demand threatens the welfare of the economy, the government can step in to provide equity.

In this system price dictates half of what, how, and for whom!

3.   THE PLAN

When using the **plan** for an economic system the choices of what is produced, how it's produced, and for whom, is decided completely by the government. This means that when the Plan is the economic system, **supply** and **demand** are **entirely absent.**

How does it work?

All of the factors of production (_____, labor, _____, natural _____) (notice what is missing is _____) are owned and controlled by the government. Because the government owns all of the means of production, they have absolute authority to answer our three questions.

Because neither supply nor demand are present, all decisions of what the economy produces (how much of it), and how (the means of production), and for whom, will be mapped out in a plan created by the government.

What are the benefits of the Plan?

- Absolute equality

- Availability of public goods

- No danger of misallocation of resources dictated by profit

- No unplanned inflation or unemployment (therefore no danger of economic swings known as the business cycle)

What are the disadvantages?

- _____

- _____

- _____

- _____

Notice that because supply and demand are non-existent, _____ is non-existent!

OPTIMALITY

Now that we have a general idea of the different choices available to an economy in answering:

- _____

- _____

- _____

. . . we can investigate which system is best.

When does anyone know when any given choice of action was successful?

_____

By that I mean, how does anyone know that what they were trying to do, worked? We usually judge success by the results, right? The results are related to the goal that was sought after. The closer the results are to the goal = the closer the results are to correct or desirable. When you paint a room in your house, you have a vision of how it will look and Viola, it is exactly as you had hoped it would be and you call your mission a success. Or perhaps you plan on making some exquisite pistachio encrusted mahi-mahi with scalloped potatoes and sautéed asparagus for dinner and wow it turns out exactly as you had expected it might. You will call this a success. In the same way we attribute success to our painted room or our sophisticated dinner menu, we can see if our economic systems choice is a success by first declaring our goal.

First we must list some of the various goals that any economy might pursue.

- _____

- _____

- _____

- _____

- If our systems goal is _____, we will call it successful when _____, and unsuccessful when _____.

- If our systems goal is _____, we will call it successful when _____, and unsuccessful when _____.

- If our systems goal is _____, we will call it successful when _____, and unsuccessful when _____.

- If our systems goal is _____, we will call it successful when _____, and unsuccessful when _____,

The optimality (best) system will be decided in accordance to how well the system meets the goals it declares.

Comparing Economic Systems

As it turns out, optimality is decided by the extent to which the declared goal is reached. It is important to notice that the optimal system is not fixed in time. As soon as the goal changes then the best way to realize the new goal may change. If the goal changes but the system stays the same and the goal is not reached, then the failure is that the wrong system was used, not the wrong goal.

To fairly compare what goals can be met with which system we will look at what each system is built to achieve and what goals the system cannot meet.

1. The Market

_____

_____

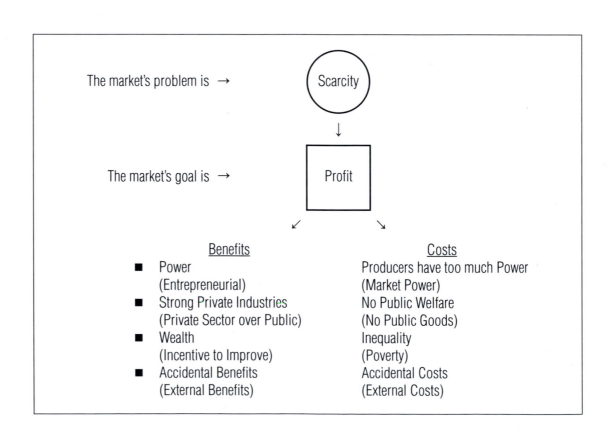

I.   MARKET POWER:

The market is tied directly to the principle of entrepreneurship, which allows for freedom to

produce and thereby _____. For producers this profit is an incentive to con-

tinue producing. For buyers, the entrepreneurial motive brings about innovative and high

quality goods and services. The trouble begins when these producers gain *too much* power in

comparison to other businesses (lack of _____). When one supplier is all that

remains (_____), the imbalance in power between supply and demand is

large enough that, at the expense of the buyer, only the supplier is benefited.

Think of different costs that may arise when the monopolist abuses his power.

■   _____

■   _____

■   _____

■   _____

II.   PUBLIC GOODS:

If producers are motivated by profit in producing goods and services, then does that mean

they will not produce those goods and services that do not generate profit?

YES

In keeping with profit as the number-one motive for producers to supply output in a market, it

is safe to assume that where profit is lacking, some goods and services will not be produced.

As soon as producers opt-out of producing certain goods or services because they are not

profitable, we will not have them in the market.

What types of goods and services are not profitable?

a. Goods and services where there are too many suppliers tend to be unprofitable. Some industries include farming and compulsory education. Another way of thinking about this is to think of those goods or services where it does not matter where you get them: water, electricity, police, elementary school, bread, and roads. While some of these goods and services are provided and profitable in the market they are "generic" in nature.

b. Goods and services where it is hard (or impossible) to enforce payment in order to consume them. An extreme example of this is national defense. If a private company serviced our national defense needs, then in order to receive the benefits of a safe society we would have to pay directly for the protection and those that did not pay would not be protected. How could that work? How would it be possible to not defend those who hadn't paid? Another example is roads; where only those that paid to use the road could travel. How would those that couldn't afford to pay get anywhere? Or how about medical care? What if you were only entitled to medical care if you could afford it? Would that mean that because of the profit motive you died if you could not afford treatment?

c. Goods and services which are necessary for all of society, but available from only one supplier.

How many different rail tracks do we need to transport cargo between California and New York? How many different energy companies do you need to connect electricity to your house? How many different telephone poles do we need? This type of industry is called a natural monopoly and is characterized by being necessary to all people but provided by only one source of supply.

Whatever the reason the good or service is not profitable it will not be produced unless the government produces it, or contracts with the private sector to have it produced. Goods and services that generate little to no profit are called public goods. A public good is easily identified by the fact that no one wants to make them and no one wants to pay for them.

III. INEQUALITY

A third consequence of the profit motive is that not all can profit. Profitability is the result of competition that results in a winner and a loser. This means that some will necessarily do better than others as long as the profit motive is running the show. In other words, there <u>will be</u> income inequality as a result of the profit motive.

How unequal are income levels in the United States?

Using a population of 300 million we divide into five equal groups of 20%. Each of our groups will be comprised of sixty million people. The richest 20% of the population earn 50% of the US income. The poorest 20%, also comprised of sixty million, earn 3.4% of the US income. To find today's US income, look up US Real GDP under the Bureau of Labor & Statistics. In _____ the Real GDP is _____. Now, multiply that number by the respective earned percentage rates to determine:

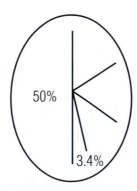

How rich is rich? _____ How poor is poor? _____.

IV. EXTERNALITIES

The final outcome of the profit motive is that it causes businesses to find the least expensive route to production in order to increase profit and decrease costs. For the buyer, this commonly results in a lower price, but a price that does not include ALL of the COSTS. Which costs are not included? The social costs that result from production which are not direct costs to the producer, but rather are external to the production process. These social costs are called external costs because they are not included in the producers' direct costs (such as land and labor). In other words, external costs are outside a producer's costs to produce. This means that someone other than the producer is burdened with the unpaid costs, usually society, and as a result the final price does not reflect the true costs of production. A common example is pollution. If a producer can save production costs by polluting the air with toxic emissions then he may. Since the market is motivated by profit, reducing costs is a key method to attaining such profit. Cost reduction will be a priority even when it may harm an unrelated third party. Without _____, the harmful behavior occurs and the cost of damage is not included in the cost of production. This is problematic for two reasons:

A. damage occurs

B. the market price is false

So far, in order to reduce the amount of unpaid external costs, the government regulates the behavior that causes the costs. They do this by levying fines and requiring permits to continue the undesirable productive processes. In so doing, the producer must pay for the fine or the permit and the price increases. The increase in price may more closely represent the external cost to society.

In comparing economic systems we can simply reverse the costs and benefits of the market to find the costs and benefits of the Plan.

2. The Plan

_____

_____

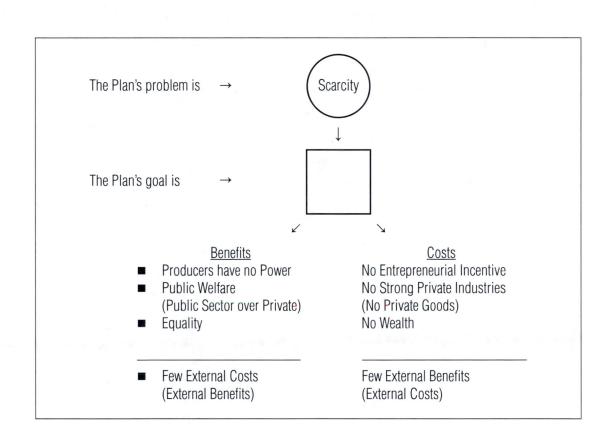

The Plan's problem is → (Scarcity)

The Plan's goal is →

Benefits	Costs
■ Producers have no Power	No Entrepreneurial Incentive
■ Public Welfare (Public Sector over Private)	No Strong Private Industries (No Private Goods)
■ Equality	No Wealth
■ Few External Costs (External Benefits)	Few External Benefits (External Costs)

3.   The Mix

_____

_____

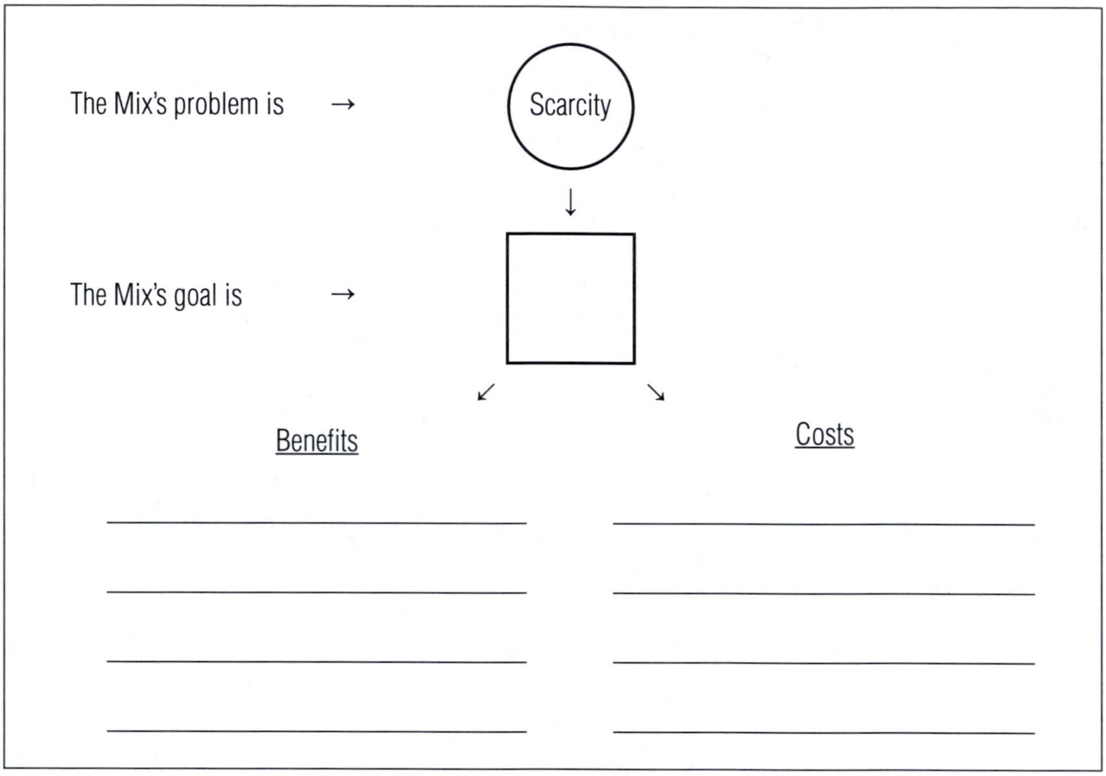

The Mix's problem is   →   (Scarcity)

↓

[ ]

↙   ↘

Benefits   Costs

The Mix's goal is   →

_____   _____

_____   _____

_____   _____

_____   _____

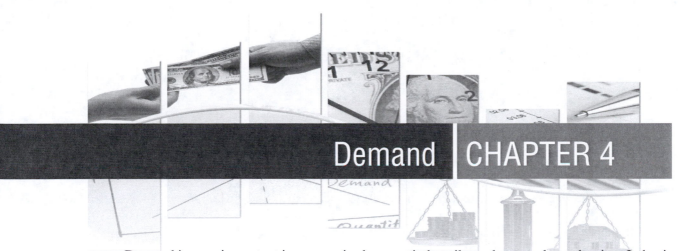

Demand | CHAPTER 4

Demand is very important in economics because it describes what people are buying. In business, this is referred to as a producer's market, or a seller's customers, or a business's demographic. There are many ways to express demand but no matter how it is said, they all essentially mean **what is being bought.**

In economics, demand means that someone is:

■ **Willing**

   (and)

■ **Able**

We will explore both separately:

■ **Willing**

In order for demand to exist you must first **WANT** the good or service in question. This may mean that you desire, wish for, and need the good or service. You may also want the good or service in relation to your demand for something else. For example, you do not consume gasoline yourself, but you buy it for your car so that you can get somewhere else. You have the desire to get somewhere and so you have the demand for gas.

■   **Able**

The second component of demand is your ability to pay. Without the money to buy something you simply want the good/service. Wanting the good does not get you the good. This is why some producers market their advertising campaigns toward children. They understand that children do not have income so they first create the *want, wish, and need* component of demand by targeting children in their ads. They hope that the children will solicit their parents, who do have the income, but until their children ask for it, are missing the willing. You can also see the able component when a salesperson asks you "How much are you able to spend?" . . . translation: "How much money do you have?" . . . how **ABLE** are you?

Once able and willing exist, a demand curve is created.

The Law of Demand

Demand curves are downward-sloping. They are downward-sloping because as you consume more of anything, your level of satisfaction diminishes. A downward-sloping line expresses an inverse (negative) relationship between what is being measured on the *Y* axis against what is being measured on the *X* axis. This negative relationship in the case of a demand curve is an inverse relationship between the price that you are willing and able to pay, and the quantity that you are willing and able to consume. Given that your level of satisfaction falls as you consume more and more of anything, the price that you are willing and able to pay must also fall to compensate for your diminished satisfaction. In other words, you are matching your satisfaction with price, and since satisfaction is _____, then what you are willing and able to pay must also _____.

The Law of Diminishing Utility (or diminishing marginal utility)

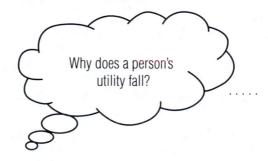

. . . Scarcity

Think about eating your favorite food. When you first sit down to eat you are very hungry. Your first bite is immensely satisfying because you are so hungry. The second bite you take is also very satisfying but not quite as much as the first. Your third bite is good but the meal is not as hot as it was when you first starting eating and the temperature change causes your level of satisfaction to decline. Nevertheless, you continue eating and with each incremental bite your hunger level decreases. By the time you take your twentieth bite you are nearly full. The empty space in your stomach has shrunk (stomach space is now _____) due to the consumption of increasing amounts of food. Eventually, you will not be able to gain any more satisfaction from eating because you are no longer hungry. Hunger is now non-existent. Satisfaction can no longer be the result of continued consumption and, in fact, satisfaction will turn negative if you continue to eat because you are full.

This phenomenon is an example of the Law of Diminishing Marginal Utility, which declares that a consumer's incremental or _____ utility will diminish (_____) with the consumption of additional units of a good/service in a given time period. The amount of additional or _____ satisfaction you get from consuming more of anything decreases when all other factors of consumption are held constant. The other factors might include _____

_____ .

The negative slope of the demand curve expresses that as quantity demanded increases; price

must fall as a result of _____ utility.

Ok, so we understand that because _____ decreases with additional units

consumed, price must _____ to compensate for the decreasing satisfaction

from additional units consumed.

Once you have both the willing and able components of demand, a demand curve exists.

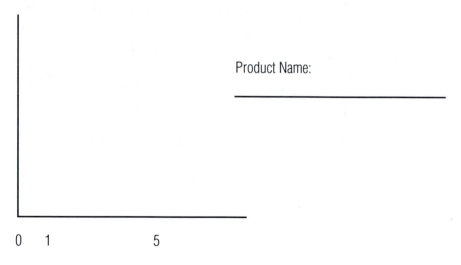

Product Name:

_____

0   1   5

■   Label the *Y* axis "*P*" for price. Label the *X* axis "*Q*" for quantity.

How much would you pay for one unit?

■   On your price axis, write the highest amount you would pay.

Imagine you are interested in buying five units of this good. You might pay the same for each of the five units as you paid for one unit, but because of the law of diminishing _____ utility, people demand a lower price in order to consume increasing quantities.

■   On your price axis and under the price you paid for the one unit, write the lowest amount (per unit) you would pay.

© Miguel Argel Salinas, 2010. Used under license from Shutterstock, Inc.

What made you interested in demanding the good or service you picked?

_____.

_____.

My guess is that you like the good or service (_____) which is the same as _____ and _____, and you knew that you could afford it (_____). It could also be that you picked it because others did

(_____). Or perhaps it was because you consider it a necessity and there is

only one supplier (_____). A final guess is that you have bought it in the past

and you enjoyed it (_____). Whatever the reason you had in mind, you picked

what you picked, because of the five factors of demand.

The Five Factors of Demand

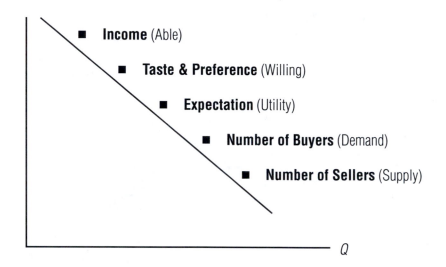

■ **Income** (Able)

■ **Taste & Preference** (Willing)

■ **Expectation** (Utility)

■ **Number of Buyers** (Demand)

■ **Number of Sellers** (Supply)

Q

1. Income

Income refers to money earned from work, interest, rent, rebates, and _____.

2. Tastes and Preference

Taste and Preference refers to a person's desire or interest in having the good or service.

3. Number of Suppliers

Number of suppliers refers to how many other producers are producing competing products

(known as _____) and those that are producing products that complement

said product (known as _____).

4. Number of Buyers

Number of buyers refers to the number of people in the market for the good/service. These buyers will make up the market demand for the product.

5. Expectations

Expectations refer to the consumers' forecasted satisfaction (known as _____ in economics) from consuming the good/service.

What were your factors of Demand?

Going back to the good or service you picked to demand, we will look at each of the factors of demand to identify the economic criteria you used in making your choice.

1. Income

_____

_____

2. Tastes and Preference

_____

_____

3. Number of Suppliers

_____

_____

4. Number of Buyers

_____

_____

5. Expectations

_____

_____

> Let's Talk About Our Demand Curve

1. What does it mean that the line is downward-sloping?

_____

2. What will happen to your demand curve if:

    a. Your income changes?

    _____

    b. Your tastes change?

    _____

    c. Your thoughts of how useful the good or service is change?

    _____

    d. The price of a good you consume this good with changes?

    _____

    e. A good you like just as much as this good goes on sale?

    _____

When any of the five factors change, the placement of the ENTIRE _____

curve may move or shift. Why? The location of the demand curve is decided by these factors

of demand. If any of these factors change, the placement of the demand curve will change. We

call this a **shift** or a **change** in demand. Think about it in terms of the conditions that you

stated for the good/service you have demand for: If any of those conditions were different,

would your demand curve be plotted differently?

Shifts in Demand

Shifts in demand occur when the circumstances of what created the demand curve in the

first place change. This means that a demand curve may shift when any factor of demand

that created the demand curve changes. If your income changes the demand curve may

shift. If your _____ and _____ for the good change, your

_____ curve may shift. If the total _____ of

_____ in the market for the good increases or _____, the de-

mand curve may shift. If there is suddenly more suppliers supplying a similar good or service,

the original market demand may shift. Finally, if your _____ for utility

changes, the demand curve may shift.

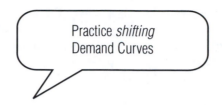

Income

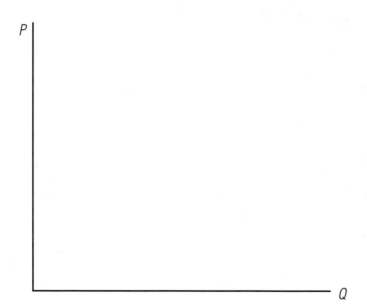

An increase in income
(affects ABLE)

Taste and Preference

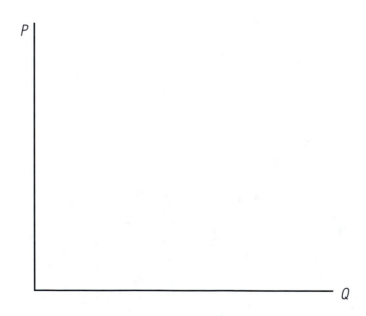

An decrease in taste
and preferences
(affects willing)

Number of Buyers

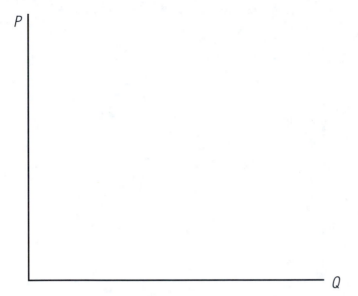

An increase in the
number of buyers
(affects the market demand)

Expectations

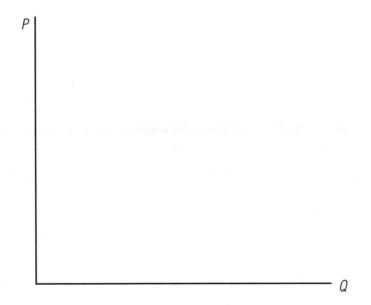

An increase in expectations
(affects utlity)

Number of Sellers

The factor of demand called the number of sellers is two-parts.

a.   **Complements**

b.   **Substitutes**

(both affect supply)

A.   Complements: A complement refers to goods that go well together: hot dogs and buns, pizza and cola, movies and popcorn. When the price of one changes and the market demand for the other shifts as a result, then the goods are considered complements. Where one good increases in price, the complementary good will show a decrease in demand. Or, where one good decreases in price, the complementary good will show an increase in demand. The impact from a price change where two goods are considered to be complements is inverse.

A decrease in the price of the complementary good

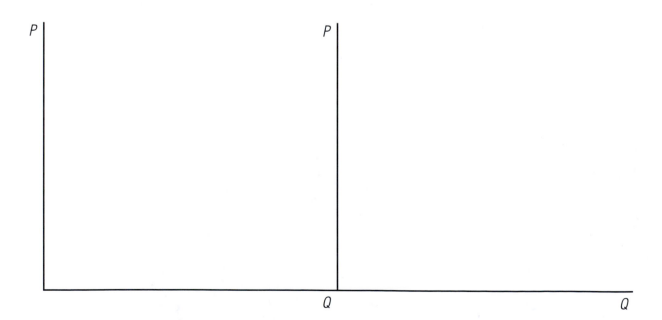

B. Substitutes: Two goods are considered substitutes when a change in the price of one good results in a change in the market demand for the other good. Substitutes could also be called competition. They are substitutes to the extent that the market demand for both goods considers the two goods to substitute well for each other. Coke and Pepsi are seen by many as substitutable; Toyota, Nissan, and Honda are seen by many as substitutable; sugar and Sweet & Low may often be used as substitutes. Where two goods are considered to be substitutes, a change in the price of one will shift the demand curve for the other in the same direction. This is a direct relationship.

A decrease in the price of a substitute good

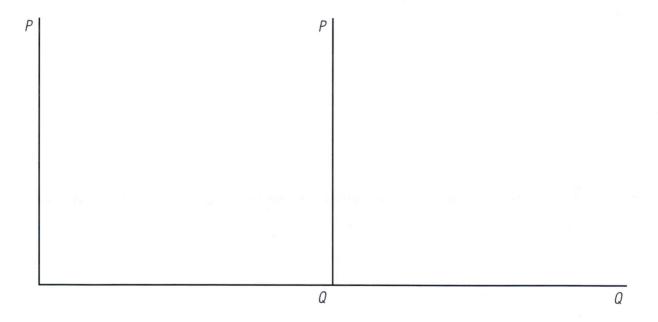

Price

You may have noticed when learning about the factors of demand, that price was NOT included as a factor of demand. What this means is that price cannot create demand.

The role that price serves is that of changing the amount of demand. This is called a change in **quantity demanded.** This means that price is only relevant **AFTER** a demand curve exists.

Price changes cause changes in Quantity Demanded

As soon as a demand curve is constructed from the factors that created it, then we can raise and lower price to see the effect on quantity demanded. The degree to which quantity demanded might change as a result of a change in price will depend upon the slope of the demand curve. This means that a change in price could change the quantity demanded by a large amount or a small amount. The degree to which quantity demanded will change from a change in price is dependent on the slope of the demand curve.

Notice that a price change means a change from an old price to a new price. Notice also that when a new price is given that the new price will affect only one new quantity amount. This means that only **one** price and **one quantity** combination is affected by a change in price, not the entire demand curve. If all price and quantity combinations change, then a shift in demand would have to have occurred. When price changes, the entire demand curve does not change, because that would be the same as changing **ALL** prices and corresponding quantities.

Price does not create Demand

A change in price will only motivate someone to purchase something if they already have

_____ . It is important to understand that measuring the change in

_____ can only occur once a demand curve exists. In other words, if you

do not want the good or service in question, or you do not have the income by which to

purchase it, then any change in price will affect nothing, because there will be no

_____ curve to affect.

This means that Price does not create demand!

If you don't believe it . . .

think of a good or service that *you want, but can't afford;* or you can think of a good or service that you *can afford, but don't want,* and plot your demand curve below.

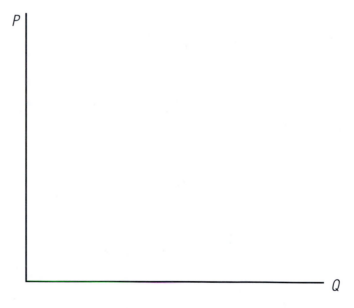

Were you able to construct a demand curve given that you did not have the income or the willingness to purchase? _____ . Good! This means that price doesn't

_____ demand.

The Role Price Serves

Draw a demand curve in the graph below identifying what you are willing and able to pay for quantities from one through ten.

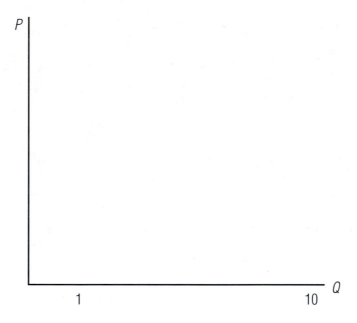

Price Elasticity of Demand

Price elasticity measures how responsive demand is to a change in price. In other words if price changed by five cents, price elasticity measures how much of a change in quantity demanded would occur. Once a demand curve exists, we can measure the rate of change of utility relative to quantity demanded resulting from a change in price. A good is elastic versus inelastic based on: how disposable the good is (i.e., is the good a necessity); how expensive the good is relative to income; how many substitutes are available; and finally, how much time a person has to adjust from consuming to not consuming. Elasticity is useful to a supplier who wishes to determine whether or not to _____ or _____ his price. Price elasticity of demand tells a producer what will happen to *his* market (already _____ demand) if he raises or lowers his price.

Where the slope is steep it means that any change on the *Y* axis (price) will be larger than any change on the *X* axis (quantity). Where the slope is nearly flat, it means the opposite; a small change in price will result in a large change in quantity.

When we discuss elasticity we are talking about how responsive any market is to a change in price. When we say that a market is very responsive, we call it price elastic. When we say a market is not responsive, we call it price inelastic.

When the good is considered price elastic, the price elasticity of demand will be greater than one. This means that when a producer raises his price, the market (or his customers) will increase or decrease the amount of demand for his product by more than the amount that he increased his price. If the price elasticity is less than one, it means that when the producer raises his price, his market will not respond by very much: The quantity of lost customers will be less than the amount by which he raises his price. Sometimes a producer can raise price by some amount, say one, and have quantity demanded change by the same amount, one. This is called unitary elastic. It means that any change in price is matched by an equal change in quantity demanded.

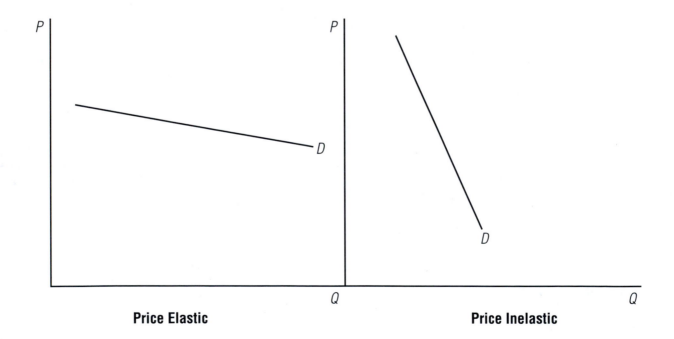

Price Elastic   **Price Inelastic**

■   On both graphs, identify two price levels and their corresponding quantities

Price Elastic: When price changes from _____ to _____,

quantity demanded changes from _____ to _____. The

change in price is less than the change in quantity demanded.

Price Inelastic: When price changes from _____ to _____,

quantity demanded changes from _____ to _____. The

change in price is greater than the change in quantity demanded.

Calculating Price Elasticity

To calculate for price elasticity, the following formula is used:

$$Pe = \%\, \blacktriangle\, QD \div \%\, \blacktriangle\, P$$

Where: Pe = Price Elasticity
% = Percent
$\blacktriangle$ = Change
QD = Quantity Demanded
P = Price

What the number means:

Is the response high or low?

When *Pe* is greater than one = Price Elastic =

_____

When *Pe* is less than one = Price Inelastic =

_____

When *Pe* is zero   = Unitary Elastic =

_____

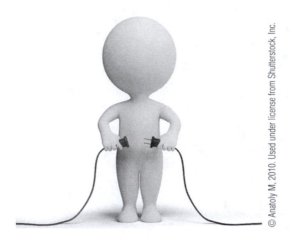

Let's calculate the Price Elasticity of Demand

We will use the numbers from our Price Elastic and Price Inelastic graphs.

We will be calculating the percent change in both quantity demanded and price. We will calculate each separately.

Percent Change In Quantity Demanded

1. Subtract your new quantity demanded amount from your old amount.

    Example:

    New Amount = 2

    Old Amount = 10

    $2 - 10 = -8$

    (The fact that QD has decreased means that price increased)

2. Add your quantity demanded amounts together and divide by 2 to get an average. We need an average amount between the two quantity demand levels to find the percent change.

Example:

$2 + 10 = 12$

$12 \div 2 = 6$

3. Finally, we will find the percent change by taking the difference between the new quantity demanded and the old quantity demanded and dividing by the average.

Example:

$-8 \div 6 = -1.3 =$ Percent change in quantity demanded.

(The fact that the answer is negative means that price increased)

Next we will do the same calculations to find the percent change in price.

Percent Change in Price

1. Subtract your new price amount from your old price.

Example:

New Price $= 6$

Old Price $= 5$

$6 - 5 = 1$

2. Add your prices together and divide by 2 to get an average. We need an average amount between the two price levels to find the percent change.

Example:

$6 + 5 = 11$

$11 \div 2 = 5.5$

3. Finally, we will find the percent change by taking the difference between the new price and the old price and dividing by the average.

Example:

$1 \div 5.5 = .1818 =$ Percent change in price.

Price Elasticity or *Pe*

To find the Price Elasticity, take your percent change in quantity demanded and divide by your percent change in price.

Example:

$-1.3 \div .1818 = 1.48$

Interpreting Your Answer

■ First of all, the negative numbers symbolize a decrease in quantity demanded from an increase in price . . . **The Law of demand!** Although the answer will always be negative when price is increased because of the law of demand, the absolute value is used to determine whether the answer is greater than, less than or equal to one.

■ Second, if your answer was greater than one (1) (absolute value), it means that the quantity demanded for that range along your demand curve is price elastic . . . which means that the market will respond by decreasing the quantity they demand by more than the amount of the price increase.

- Third, the *Pe* number you are left with describes the change in quantity demanded from a one unit change in price.

Example:

Pe = −1.48 means that for the range calculated there will be a 1.48 percent loss in quantity demanded for every one unit increase in price.

Price Elastic vs. Price Inelastic

Goods and services will be more price elastic than price inelastic when the following conditions are present:

- The good has many substitutes
- The good is not a necessity
- People have time to adjust their behavior

Income Elasticity

Income elasticity is similar to price elasticity except that instead of changing price and watching what happens to quantity demanded, income elasticity measures what happens to the entire demand curve when income levels change. Remember, income is a factor of demand and therefore any change in income levels should make the demand curve **shift.** Income elasticity measurements tell a producer how demand for all price and quantity combinations will change relative to a change in consumer income.

The demand for all goods and services will not increase or decrease from any given change in income in the same way. The shift in demand is dependant upon the good.

Rules:	Increase in Income	Types
Normal Good:	Demand will shift out and to the right	_____
Superior Good:	Demand will shift out and to the right	_____
Inferior Good:	Demand will shift in and to the left	_____

When the income elasticity is greater than zero but less than one

. . . Normal good: inelastic

When the income elasticity is greater than one

. . . Superior good: elastic

When the income elasticity is less than zero

. . . Inferior good: negative inelastic

The formula used to measure how much demand will shift by is given as:

$$Yed = \% \blacktriangle QD \div \% \blacktriangle Income$$

Where *Yed*:	Income Elasticity
%:	Percent
σ:	Change
Income:	Disposable Income

Key: Remember that although we are using a change in quantity demanded to measure the shift in demand, we are holding prices constant. This means that the result describes how much demand shifts from a change in income, given that prices are constant.

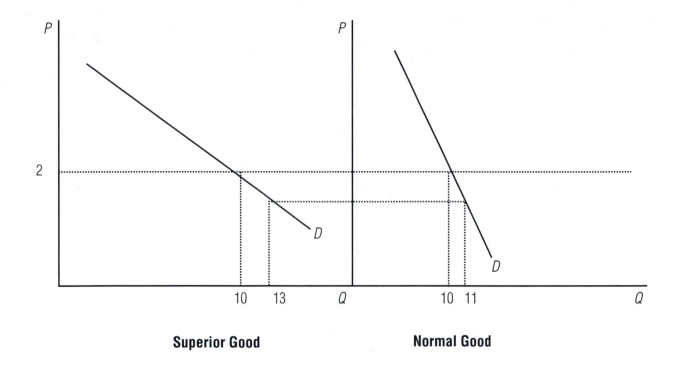

Superior Good   **Normal Good**

Using the graphs above, we will hold price constant at 2 and evaluate the percent change in quantity demand when income increases from $40,000 to $50,000.

Quantity demanded increases from   Quantity demanded increases from

_____ to _____   _____ to _____

Let's calculate the percent change in income first since it is the same for both graphs.

Percent Change in Income

1. First, subtract your old income from your new income.

_____

2. Next, add your income levels together and divide by two to get an average.

_____

3. Finally, divide the difference in your income by your average.

_____

Your percent change in income is _____.

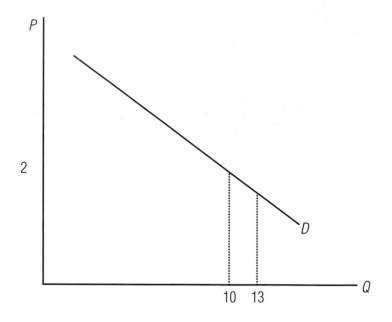

Percent Change in Quantity Demanded for the Superior Good

1. First subtract your old quantity demanded from your new quantity demanded.

_____

2. Next, add your quantity demanded levels together and divide by two to get an average.

_____

3. Finally divide the difference in your quantity levels by your average.

_____

Your percent change in Quantity Demanded is _____.

Yed **To calculate the income elasticity, divide your percent change in quantity**

demanded by your percent change in income. _____

Yed = _____ **and is therefore a** _____ **good, because it is**

_____ **than one.**

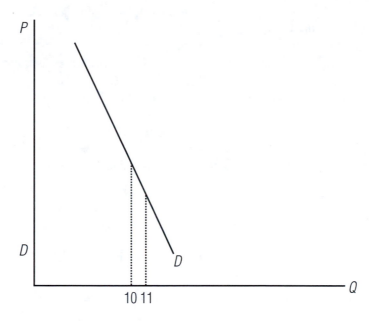

Percent Change in Quantity Demanded for the Normal Good

1. First subtract your old quantity demanded from your new quantity demanded.

_____

2. Next, add your quantity demanded levels together and divide by two to get an average.

_____

3. Finally divide the difference in your quantity levels by your average.

_____

Your percent change in Quantity Demanded is _____.

Yed **To calculate the income elasticity, divide your percent change in quantity de**

manded by your percent change in income. _____

Yed = _____ **and is therefore a _____ good, because it is**

_____ **than one.**

Cross Price Elasticity

Cross price elasticity is a final way to measure a consumer response to a change in price. Cross price elasticity tells you what may happen to your market when another supplier changes their price. If the other supplier is producing a good that complements what your market produces, then their change will cause an inverse change in your market.

If, on the other hand, the other supplier is your competition (substitute), whatever they do will result in a direct change in your market. If they raise their price, your market will increase. If they lower their price, your market will decrease.

Why is this a valuable measurement?

If you are a producer and what you believe to be your competition and your demand (your market) is unchanged, then you know that the market you serve does not see the other supplier as a substitute for your product. However, if there is a change in the demand you serve, then you can price accordingly. We will investigate your options later, but for now, let's see how it works.

Suppose you produce Soda X and you want to know if the market sees Soda Y as your competition. Soda Y raises its price from $1.00 to $1.25. When this happens the demand for your Soda X changes from five to ten. Using these numbers, calculate the price elasticity of demand for Soda X using the following formula.

Cross Price Elasticity Formula: $CPe = \% \triangle QD\,x \div \% \triangle P\,y$

$$CPe = \text{Cross Price Elasticity}$$
$$Triangle\ symbol = \text{Change}$$
$$QD = \text{Quantity Demanded}$$
$$x = \text{good } X$$
$$P = \text{Price}$$
$$y = \text{good Y}$$

Percent Change in Quantity Demanded

1. Subtract the old *QD* from the new *QD*.

    _____

2. Add the *QD* amounts together and divide by 2 to get an average.

    _____

3. Take the difference in your *QD* amount and divide by your average.

    _____

Percent Change in Price

1. Subtract the old price from the new price.

    _____

2. Add the prices together and divide by 2 to get an average.

    _____

3. Take the difference in your price levels and divide by your average.

    _____

Cross Price Elasticity

Divide the percent change in *QD* by the percent change in Price. _____

Cross Price Elasticity Rule Book

Where the answer is positive, the two goods are considered substitutes.

Where the answer is negative the two goods are complements.

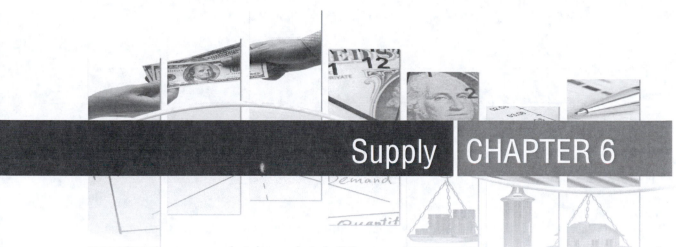

Supply means <u>what is produced</u>. When producers produce, they are producing supply. Sometimes supply is called output; sometimes supply is called quantity. We label output with a "*Q*" on a graph. The "*Q*" is representative of quantity. Quantity is always what is being measured on the "*x*" axis on a given graph.

A producer is the one who is producing output. A producer will produce output when he can afford what it costs to produce and when he is interested in producing this output. The words we associate with a producer's **interest** and **ability** to produce are _____ and _____ .

I. WILLING

Willing can be described as interest. What makes a producer interested in producing in one market over another? If you have established that you can afford (_____) to produce, the next reasonable question to answer is "do I want to?" I am sure you can think of plenty of things you could do but are not interested in doing. So let's think about what might affect how *Willing* (interested) you are to produce?

List what factors you think might motivate a person to start a business?

_____

_____

_____

_____

_____

_____

There are economic words associated with everything that you listed above that all establish how motivated or interested a producer is in producing output.

The Factors of Supply for "Willing"

Below are some of the main factors that create the "willingness" to supply output. Description:

■ Number of Buyers

_____

■ Number of Other Sellers

_____

■ Expectations

_____

Ok, great! So given you could afford to do a job (_____) and you were _____ in doing the job, then you will probably succeed in doing what you are setting out to do, right?

1. Number of Buyers: This is your market demand. These are the number of customers you might be selling to.

_____

2. Number of Other Sellers: This one is a little tricky because it is two-fold. On the one hand it describes how many other current suppliers there are supplying mostly the same thing you want to supply. This is generally referred to as your _____. We will save the entire conversation of competition for the chapter entitled "Market Structure," but nonetheless, how much competition exists will most certainly be a very large factor when it comes to deciding whether to enter the market or not.

    The number of sellers also describes those businesses that are suppliers of goods and services that "go with" your product. Products or services that "go with" your product or service are generally referred to as _____. Whether or not your product or service comes with many or few complements will have an impact on your willingness to supply. Complements are measured by elasticity.

3. Expectations: This is the final factor that will be a consideration before supply exists. The word "expectations" is defined as:

    1. a confident belief or strong hope that a particular event will happen

    2. a mental image of something expected, often compared to its reality (often used in the plural)

    3. a standard of conduct or performance expected by or of somebody (often used in the plural)

    4. somebody's likely prospects of wealth or success in the future

In economics the belief over an event occurring usually refers to profit. It could be profit in terms of money, safety, wealth, happiness, or any other desired outcome. The role that people's beliefs have on any given outcome is one that is discussed in a vast number of behavioral sciences, including anthropology, sociology, psychology, and economics. What each of these

Encarta® World English Dictionary © 1999 Microsoft Corporation. All rights reserved. Developed for Microsoft by Bloomsbury Publishing Plc.

disciplines share is how humans behave. In economics expectations cause action. The action could be a shift (_____) of the supply curve. We will develop in greater detail which way the supply curve moves depending on people's expectations, but for now suffice it to say that when expectations for profit on any level exist, suppliers are more willing to supply.

II.   ABLE

Given that the above factors are in place a producer is probably interested in producing output. But that is NOT ENOUGH. Just because you want to do something does not mean you can, right?! What might affect how ABLE you are to produce?

_____

An economist describes supply (output, or "Q") as the amount a producer is able to supply given the variables he faces in producing that output.

The Factors of Supply for "Able"

The factors that create the "ability" to supply output (Q) include:

Description:

- Factor Costs

_____

- Regulation

_____

- Taxes/Subsidies

_____

Once the _____ to produce is connected with the _____ to produce, output or Q will be created. It is extremely important to note that a producer will ONLY produce when he is both _____ and _____ to produce.

Able = The Costs of Production

The costs of production are the first issue to talk about when it comes to the ability to supply. Think about it, if you are about to do something, don't you think you have already considered all the costs to do it? Producers are no different. Before any producer begins production they have mapped out what it is going to cost to do it. The discussion of these costs is broken down into sections and graphs. By the end of the chapter you will understand what goes into a producer's costs, item by item.

■ **FIXED COST**

Work with a buddy and think of a product the two of you could make.

1. Your product or service is _____

2. Ok, next think of some costs that you will have to pay just to open and start your business. In economics, these are called fixed costs. Fixed costs are costs that you incur just to open up your business. These are the cost you have to pay just to get started, even though no output is produced. (Hint: Think of those things that you have to pay as overhead.)

Item	Cost

Total Fixed Cost _____

3. When you total out all of these fixed costs they are the costs that you will incur just to start business.

Remember: Paying these costs does not create output, and that means they are FIXED COSTS. (No _____ increases or decreases because you paid your Fixed Costs!)

4. Where are you going to get the money to start this business and pay your fixed costs? _____ at a rate of _____ percent.

5. Take the total amount you calculated as fixed cost and divide by 365. This number will be the total amount of fixed cost you will pay per day through the year.

_____

6. Now we are going to graph these daily fixed costs. On the empty graph below, assign numbers to the *Y* axis that identify a range of cost figures. If your total cost from the table you completed was $200.00, for example, you can mark costs of 50, 100, 150, and 200 on the graph below.

7. Next you will draw a horizontal line from the *Y* axis straight across. Label the line you construct as Fixed Cost.

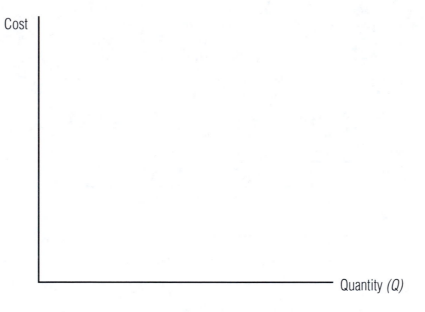

So far we have calculated what this business will spend just to start business. That means that all of the costs paid so far have not resulted in creating any output.

■ **VARIABLE COST**

Are you ready to create some Output??

In order to create output (Q), we are going to have to "take on" some variable costs. Variable costs will include those costs that will cause a change in output. This means that we will have to hire some _____ and get some other _____. Because we can alter both, they are the most typical example of variable costs that we have to pay in order to start production.

Variable Costs defined:

_____

_____

To figure out what we will need to pay to create output we can start with labor first because it is the most common variable cost.

# of Workers	Wage/Worker	Other Resources	Output Created	Variable Cost
1	$10	1	5	$11
2	$20	2	15	$22
3	$30	3	28	$33
4	$40	4	43	$44
5	$50	5	61	$55
6	$60	6	81	$66
7	$70	7	96	$77
8	$80	8	106	$88
9	$90	9	111	$99
10	$100	10	115	$110

Explaining the above table:

1. Worker #1 is paid $10.

2. Worker #2 is also paid $10. The reason the number is $20, is because that is the total cost paid for labor when two workers are used.

3. The *other* resources column defines any other resource that we could vary in order to increase or decrease output.

4. As a result of using workers and other resources, we create a certain amount of output.

5. When we calculate the amount of workers cost with the other resources cost, we can create our variable cost.

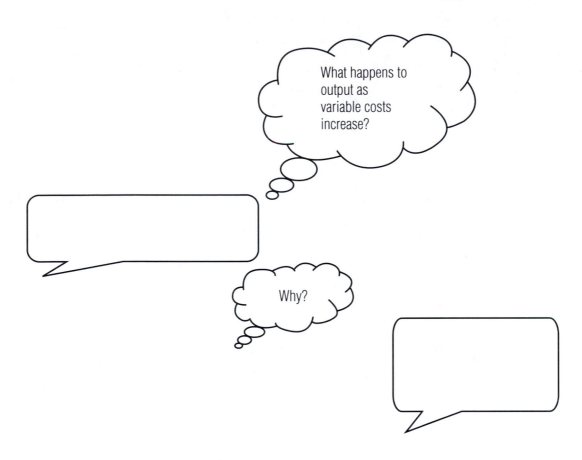

Go back and look at the fixed cost amount you decided before and add it to the table below.

Complete the Total Cost column by adding each Fixed Cost amount with each Variable Cost.

# of Workers	Output Created	Variable Cost	Fixed Cost	Total Cost
1	5	$11	$	$
2	15	$22	$	$
3	28	$33	$	$
4	43	$44	$	$
5	61	$55	$	$
6	81	$66	$	$
7	96	$77	$	$
8	106	$88	$	$
9	111	$99	$	$
10	115	$110	$	$

■   What is causing total cost to increase? _____

Recap *Definitions* of the Cost Curves:

A. Fixed Cost:

The fixed cost curve is flat because no matter how many units are produced, fixed costs stay the same. Another way of thinking about this is that fixed costs must be _____ even though _____ output is produced. Fixed costs do not change with an increase or a decrease in output. Think about it in terms of a producer who wants to crush cans for a living. In order to start production, he rents a building. He pays the landlord $1,000.00. He goes to the building on Monday morning and opens the door. There is no output produced. In fact, the building is absolutely empty, even though he paid his money. The rent is known in economics as a fixed cost.

B. Variable Cost:

Variable cost identifies those costs that are incurred in producing greater and greater levels of output.

TOTAL COST

Total cost is easy!! It is simply the sum of all fixed and variable costs. The total cost curve identifies how much a supplier can expect to pay to produce output.

Ok, we now have a clear understanding of *FC* (fixed cost), *VC*, (variable cost), and *TC* (total cost). A producer will calculate these costs to decide if he is able to provide output just simply by how much it costs him to produce.

What does the information tell a producer?

- _____

- _____

What does this information **not** tell a producer?

- _____

To figure out how much a producer should produce, economists look to see at what point the costs to produce are no longer *worth it!*

Fixed and variable costs are too large to identify when a producer is spending more money in production over what he will get back in a sale. A producer will have to identify the exact level where it will cost him more to produce than he will get back in revenue. This is the same thing as knowing whether it is a good or bad idea before you act. If you could decide a course of action before you acted knowing exactly what it would cost you before you paid for it, wouldn't you want that information? Anyone would want to know the outcome before they make a decision to prevent making a bad decision, right? Economists look at the marginal cost (the incremental cost) in order to decide when their decision is bad, or when to stop producing. A producer looks at his incremental costs to decide how many units he should produce.

MARGINAL COST

The Marginal Cost (*MC*) identifies how much it costs to produce each unit as more labor and resources are bought in order to increase output.

MC = The Change in Total Cost/The Change in Output "*Q*"

L	Q	FC	VC	TC	▲TC ÷	▲Q =	MC
0	0	$50	$0	$50	$50	0	0
1	15	$50	$100	$150	$100	15	$6.7
2	50	$50	$200	$250	$100	35	$2.85
3	125	$50	$300	$350	$100	75	$1.33
4	205	$50	$400	$450	$100	80	$1.25
5	288	$50	$500	$550	$100	83	$1.20
6	369	$50	$600	$650	$100	81	$1.23
7	444	$50	$700	$750	$100	75	$1.33
8	474	$50	$800	$850	$100	30	$3.33
9	484	$50	$900	$950	$100	10	$10
10	490	$50	$1000	$1050	$100	6	$16

KEY

L = Labor
Q = Quantity Produced
FC = Fixed Cost
VC = Variable Cost
TC = Total Cost

Change in TC ÷ Change in Q = MC

Marginal cost tells a producer how the per unit cost of production is changing. Per unit costs change with additional units produced because variable costs are increasing. That should explain why marginal cost curve follows the variable cost curve.

You might be wondering why costs just don't continue falling, right?? Why doesn't the cycle of increased output causing costs to fall continue forever? *First of all, with the exception of the unknown, all that is known always ends. MC* is no exception. Incremental costs will rise as producers get closer and closer to capacity; Marginal Physical Product explains why.

Marginal Physical Product

Marginal physical product (*MPP*) is the additional output created by one worker. With zero workers your *MPP* is zero. When you add one worker, the change in your output from nothing to the new amount created is your Marginal Physical Product amount. The entire reason that *MPP* increased was due to hiring the first worker. Before you hired him, your output was zero right? Well, then the question to ask is "Will this worker continue to add output to the total output amount?"—and the answer is no! At some point, his marginal output is going to fall and the reason why is explained by DIMINISHING MARGINAL RETURNS.

DMR means that after some point all returns (_____) will no longer increase but will decrease. Oh sure, in the beginning like most things, your first worker will increase output at a rate that is beneficial to you as he becomes skilled or proficient in what he is doing but eventually his marginal output falls because, as they say, "all good things must come to an end." Production is no different. Think about it: Unless you are constantly retraining your workers or increasing the variable resources he has to work with… there is only so much he can do . . . right? His contribution to total output is going to decline when the other variables that he has to work with do not _____ alongside him. Or maybe more simply, his energy level is falling. Maybe the coffee breaks are not doing it for him; or maybe he is tired. No matter the reason, at some point, a worker's marginal contribution to total output will no longer _____ unless all other variables that the worker uses to create output increase at the same or even at an increasing rate. This means that if a producer wants output to continue to increase per worker, he must continuously add variable inputs in the right combinations to do so. Since all resources are _____, this increase in *MPP* is a producer's largest challenge. It is because of the *MPP* decrease, that *MC* increases.

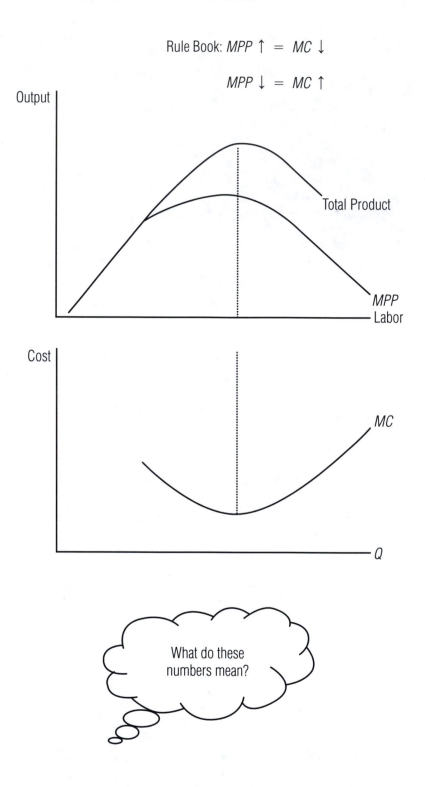

Rule Book: $MPP \uparrow = MC \downarrow$

$MPP \downarrow = MC \uparrow$

What do these numbers mean?

1. For the first _____ units produced, marginal cost is _____.

    For the next _____ units produced, marginal cost falls to

    _____ . The reason the incremental cost falls is the additional output produced is increasing at a faster rate than the increased rate of costs. This causes the additional units produced to be less and less costly because the speed of new production is faster than the speed of the new costs.

2. After some time, the marginal cost levels out. It is at this point that marginal costs are at their lowest point. This level is called the least cost production level.

   A. After the bottom out point, the marginal cost curve will begin its ascent.

   B. Marginal costs increase after the bottom out point because the additional costs of production (variable costs) are increasing at a faster rate than the additional rate of output increases.

After a producer has been in production for a period of time he might want to know about his general costs. In economics, we call the general costs of production *average costs*. We can calculate averages for all costs (and we do) with the exception of marginal cost. Marginal cost is the per unit cost and the per unit cost does not need an average.

Average Costs

a. Average Fixed Costs (*AFC*)

Take the Total Fixed Cost amount for each level and divide by quantity.

b. Average Variable Costs (*AVC*)

Take the Total Variable Cost amount for each level and divide by quantity.

c. Average Total Costs (*ATC*)

Take the Total Cost amount and divide by quantity.

With respect to averages there are some important relationships to highlight.

■   The *AFC* is downward sloping because _____ .

_____

_____

■   The *ATC* curve is U Shaped because _____ .

_____

_____

■   The *MC* curve cuts through the lowest part of the *AVC*.

_____

_____

AVERAGE COST

All average costs are calculated by dividing the cost by quantity.

a.   Average Fixed Costs (*AFC*)

Take the Total Fixed Cost amount for each level and divide by quantity.

b.   Average Variable Costs (*AVC*)

Take the Total Variable Cost amount for each level and divide by quantity.

c.   Average Total Costs (*ATC*)

Take the Total Cost amount and divide by quantity.

Workers	Output	Variable	AVC	Fixed Cost	AFC	Total Cost	ATC
1	5	$11	$	$	$	$	$
2	15	$22	$	$	$	$	$
3	28	$33	$	$	$	$	$
4	43	$44	$	$	$	$	$
5	61	$55	$	$	$	$	$
6	81	$66	$	$	$	$	$
7	96	$77	$	$	$	$	$
8	106	$88	$	$	$	$	$
9	111	$99	$	$	$	$	$
10	115	$110	$	$	$	$	$

TIME FRAME AND COST: THE SHORT RUN VS. THE LONG RUN

The Long Run

What can anyone ever say for a fact about the long run? For example, *are you definitely going to be around tomorrow? Or, for that matter, even in the next minute?* What do we really know about anything for a fact past this moment? _____. Economists characterize not knowing anything for a fact as the long run. The long run is where anything could happen because everything is variable. In the long run, nothing is fixed and everything is variable: There are no fixed costs in the long run.

The Short Run

In the short run, you know ONE thing for sure... You are there. You are fixed in the short run. The short run is the production period where at least one factor cost is fixed. This means that the producer is obliged to pay the cost regardless of how much output he produces. Using our previous example, the only thing you know for a fact in the present moment is that you are here. You are the fixed cost. The difference between the long run and the short run is simple: If a producer must pay at least ONE fixed cost, he is in the short run. The reason the distinction matters is that you do not want to make the mistake of thinking you do not have fixed costs when you really do! If you think you are free to vary all of your costs then your profit maximization point (we will explain this later) will be wrong.

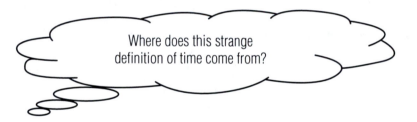

Economics originates from the discipline of philosophy. Economics has borrowed the philosophical understanding of the long run (nothing is fixed or known beyond the present moment) and translated it to distinguish long and short run costs—there are no fixed costs in the long run and there is at least one fixed cost in the short run—philosophically, "the only thing you know for sure in the present moment is that you are there."

Notes

_____

_____

_____

All Costs Together

_____ _____ are the new costs that come from using one extra variable factor. Marginal costs are created by any _____ costs incurred. These *MC* are going to increase as a result of a decrease in _____ _____. Along side increasing *MC*, the producer must pay his fixed _____. Remember, fixed costs do not _____ with an additional amount of output produced. When we add fixed costs with variable costs we have total costs. We can then take each cost separately and divide by total output to find the average of each one. Let's look at how all these curves look on a graph.

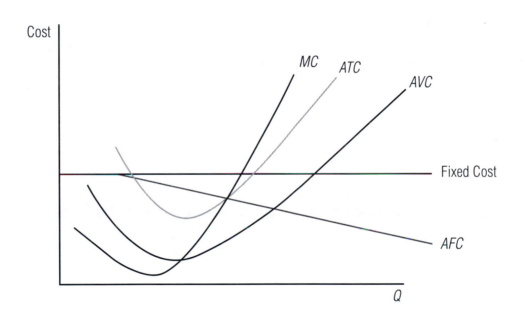

Let's talk about the relationships between these curves:

_____

_____

_____

_____

_____

_____

To conclude our cost/able portion:

On Monday, he paid $1,000.00 toward the rent on his building but produced no output.

The $1,000.00 was his fixed cost because _____.

On Tuesday, he decides to buy a machine to crush the cans. He pays $500.00 for the machine. He turns the machine on and waits for the machine to crush cans. The machine makes noises and sounds real good but does not crush any cans. The machine is also a

_____.

On Wednesday, he realizes that he could hire his friend who is very handy with machines. He pays the friend $10.00 per hour to come and work for him. His friend comes and begins work. At the onset, the friend has a lot of room to work with and is producing more crushed cans than he will be paid for: this is where *MPP* is _____ than *MC*. The second hour, the worker crushes more cans than in the first hour. Total product is

_____. Marginal Physical Product is _____. *MC* is

_____ because the cost of the worker relative to his increasing output is

_____. The Average Fixed Cost in the second hour of work is

_____ because the increase in the number of crushed cans (*TP*) will be spread out among the fixed cost as payment. The *AVC* during the second hour of work is also

_____ because *MPP* is _____. During the third hour the worker crushes more cans than he did in the second hour but the rate of change between the first and the second hour is greater than the rate of change between the second and the third hour. The worker has _____ total product, but at a _____ rate. By the fourth hour, the machine jams. The time spent to fix the machine causes the additional output, *MPP*, to _____. During this fourth hour the worker crushes as many cans as he did in hour three. Total product has _____; *MPP* has stayed the same, *MC* is at its lowest point, *AVC* is also at it lowest point, and this is where the *MC* curve

_____ the *AVC* curve. During hour number five, the worker grows tired and is

hungry and is crushing the same number of cans as he did in hour number one. *MPP* has

_____. At this point *MC* begins its _____ climb. *MPP*

will continue to _____ in relation to the number of hours worked and *MC* will

continue to _____ .

Think of some ways a producer can maintain an increase in *MPP,* and a decrease in *MC*.

_____

_____

_____

_____

More Costs

In addition to the different costs a producer faces in deciding how much to supply, producers

also must look at the regulation that exists in the market they are entering as well as the tax

level.

Regulation

According to the Encarta World English Dictionary, *Regulation* means 1. an official rule, law,

or order stating what may or may not be done; or 2. how something must be done (often used

in the plural), or the adjusting, organizing, or controlling of something, or the state of being

adjusted, organized, or controlled; or 3. an order issued by a government department or agency that has the force of law (Encarta® World English Dictionary © 1999 Microsoft Corporation. All rights reserved. Developed for Microsoft by Bloomsbury Publishing Plc).

Any time rules must be followed, resources are used to make sure they are followed. If a producer is forced to comply with rules relating to production, their costs will be affected. What might make costs increase? Producers who have to pay attention to following rules and protocol will have to file the right paper work, use certain machines, or dispose of products and waste in a certain way. Anytime behavior is monitored, costs increase.

How do regulation costs find their way into supply?

- An increase in costs shifts the entire supply curve backwards.
- A leftward shift of the supply curve means every unit produced costs more.
- The greater the regulation the harder it is to enter the market

When we deal with market structure later in the book you will see that there is a direct relationship between the degree to which a market is regulated and the number of suppliers in that market because the higher the regulation, the higher the costs; the higher the costs, the more expensive it is to enter; the more expensive it is to enter, the fewer the entries.

Taxes

There are several tax categories that businesses must pay that affect their costs.

The following are the titles to some basic taxes all businesses must pay. Depending on the structure of the business, however, some businesses will pay different levels as well as different types.

Excise Taxes

_____

_____

Property Tax

_____

_____

Gross Receipt Tax

_____

_____

Business Income Taxes

_____

_____

Sales Tax

_____

_____

Self Employment Tax

_____

_____

Payroll Tax

_____

_____

Franchise Tax

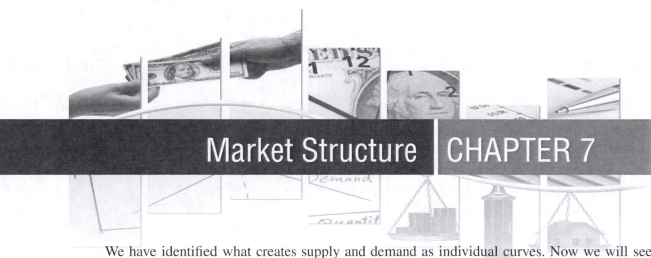

We have identified what creates supply and demand as individual curves. Now we will see what happens when we put them together. To understand what happens when supply and demand meet it is important to remember what each curve is like on their own.

- Remember that demand is created by _____ and _____.

- Remember that supply is created by _____ and _____.

- Consider that demand is comprised of consumers.

- Supply is comprised of producers.

- The demand curve is _____ sloping.

- The supply curve is _____ sloping.

> **Market Quantity is established by where Supply and Demand meet.**
>
> **Market Price is established by the price that people are willing and able to pay for the existing market quantity.**

If we know where supply and demand meet, then we will know what the market price and quantity levels are. The next question to answer then is:

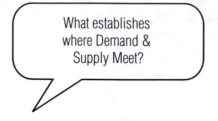

The Demand Curve

We discovered that the demand curve represents the opportunity cost a consumer has when they say they are able and willing. We defined opportunity cost as what you give up to get something else. We said that a consumer's opportunity cost will be large when:

a. the good is a necessity

b. the good is not easily substituted with another good

c. the consumer lacks the time necessary to find an alternative

When all three of the components above are present, the good is considered to be price inelastic. Recall what it means to be price inelastic.

Price Inelastic means:

_____

_____

When a good or service is price inelastic, the demand curve will be _____

_____ .

Draw a price inelastic demand curve.

If a good is not price inelastic but is the other extreme, we call it Price Elastic. When a good is price elastic it means that a consumer's opportunity cost is small. A consumer's opportunity cost will be small when:

a.   The good is a necessity but there are many substitutes.

b.   The consumer has time to find an alternative.

List some goods that are price elastic:

1.   _____

2.   _____

3.   _____

When a good or service is price elastic, the demand curve will be _____

_____ .

Draw a price elastic demand curve.

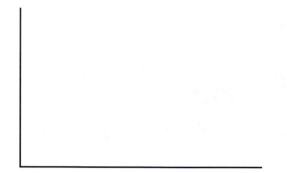

A demand curve will be drawn according to how _____ or

_____ the good in question is.

Ok, so the next question is:

What creates
Price Elasticity?

The Supply Curve

Recall the definition of supply: _____

A supplier is _____ and _____ to supply his good or service

given the variables that exist. The variables will include:

a. The _____ of _____

b. _____ of sellers, or competition and compliments

c. _____ of _____ , or demand

d. _____

e. _____ and subsidies

f. Expectations for _____

Ok, so the above variables will decide if a supplier is able and willing to supply his good or service and all of these variables make up the supply curve that is drawn. This means that the supply curve is a description of the variables in place given the conditions that created it. Again, those conditions are:

a. How big is my market? (demand)

b. How many competitors do I have? (supply)

c. How much will it cost me? (costs of production)

d. What are the taxes? (taxes)

e. How regulated is the market? (how much oversight do I have to adhere to)

f. Can I be paid to produce? (subsidies)

g. How much money do I expect to earn? (expectations)

Once a producer has the answers to these questions in place and he decides that he is going to produce, then the supply curve he constructs is a result of the answers to these questions. In other words, when and if the answers to any of these questions change, the placement, and even the very existence of the supply curve, will be different.

The market structure that the supplier is in will answer many of the questions he is asking. This means that before a supplier even begins production, some of the answers are already answered. In general, whatever the answers are will dictate how much money (profit) the potential supplier stands to earn.

This means that the shape of a producers supply curve is, in part, out of his control depending on the answers to the questions. These questions are answered in part (that is to say, a supplier's supply curve is somewhat already drawn for him) based on the market he is seeking to enter. In microeconomics, the template for the slope of a suppliers' supply curve is called Market Structure.

Market Structure

When you study economics you will notice that it is a favorite pastime to put things into categories. We do this because the study is really a study of human behavior, and given that there are so many variables to human behavior it becomes necessary to categorize in order to simplify. For example, when we talk about scarcity we describe that everything is scarce. Because "everything" is a large category, we simplify "everything" into categories. If you recall, these categories are:

a. _____

b. _____

c. _____

d. _____

e. _____

Great, I am glad you remembered what everything is. Ok, so just like we categorize everything in economics, in Microeconomics there is a categorization that describes a supplier's supply curve: The supply curve that exists depends on the answers to our supply questions.

There are five categories to describe a supply curve. Those categories are:

1. Perfect Competition

2. Monopolistic Competition

3. Oligopoly

4. Monopoly

5. Natural Monopoly

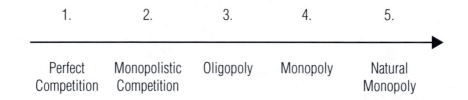

Over the next five sections, each of these categories will be described according to their templates. All five categories will define the answers to the following distinctions:

Market Structure Distinctions:

- The number of sellers in the market (competition, existing suppliers of a like product)

- The degree to which the product is unique or distinguished (diversification)

- How expensive it is to enter the market (largely in terms of fixed costs)

- The slope of the demand curve (how many customers you might gain)

- The knowledge they have regarding their competitors (how easy it is to know what your competitor is doing, largely in terms of price)

Perfect Competition

Perfect Competition

The Perfectly Competitive market structure is easily categorized by:

Many Other Suppliers (Lots of Competition)

_____

Homogenous Product (Not Unique)

_____

Low Fixed Costs

_____

A Near Horizontal Demand Curve

_____

Accurate and Easy to Obtain Information about Competitors

_____

Many Sellers

A person might enter a perfectly competitive market simply because it is easy (cheap and little to no regulation). Because it is so easy to enter hundreds do. That is why the number of sellers in this structure is the largest of the five structures.

Homogenous Product (Not Unique)

In the perfectly competitive model, the product sold is mostly the same no matter who sells it.

Low Fixed Costs

This is an easy market to enter in part because it is so cheap to start business. Economics defines cheap as one hundred thousand dollars or less.

A Near Horizontal Demand Curve

Remember the role of Demand when it comes to making money. The demand curve a producer sees is his revenue. In the case of perfect competition, the demand curve is flat. What does a flat demand curve mean? Think back to elasticity. . . .

_____

_____

_____

This means that no matter what the good intentions of the supplier are, the demand curve is so responsive (the consumers have all of the power), the supplier in a perfectly competitive market will take what he can get. If he raises price he will _____ his market because consumers will buy from the next identical supplier. If he lowers price he will go out of business because he will not be able to pay his costs. Essentially, the perfect competitor has no power to change his price because there is too much competition.

Accurate and Easy to Obtain Information about Competitors

Finally, the information that a supplier might want to have about his competition is readily available. This is because the product he is making is no different from his competitor. As a result of the fact that everyone is making the same thing, their costs are mostly the same. If their costs are nearly the same and their product is nearly the same, then there really isn't any room for secrets.

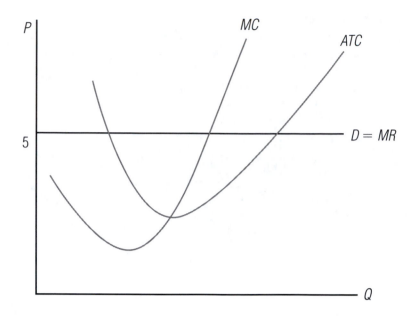

The Flat Demand Curve:

The perfect competitor faces a flat demand curve. This means that he has no _____ over price because _____ is set by the _____ _____ for what he is selling. The market demand sets the price for everything in this market. This means that the demand curve has more power than the supply curve. The reason the market demand sets price is because there is nothing unique about the supplier's product that a buyer could not get from virtually any other source.

Ok good, so we have covered why the demand curve is _____ elastic in a perfectly competitive market and since the costs in this market are duplicated between suppliers, the demand curve wins in terms of price.

The Bottom Line

Constant *MR*

Because price is flat, the perfect competitor will earn the same price no matter how many additional units he sells. This means that he cannot increase what is called marginal revenue, the additional revenue obtained from selling one more unit. Check to see if this is true. For one unit, the price is five. The change in revenue is from zero (when he sells no output) to five, the amount he earns on one unit. When he sells the second unit for price = five, the change in revenue between the first and second unit is still five.

Profit Maximization Point of Production

There are two considerations to determine the profit maximization point of production: How much output should the producer produce, and what should he charge? In the case of the perfect competitor, _____ is set for him, so the only question to answer is how many units should he produce? Look at the *MC* curve. All units on the *MC* curve represent the additional costs incurred to increase output. As long as the additional cost to produce these units is less than what the producer will gain in their sale, he will profit. So the profit maximization point is to produce up until the point where the additional costs to produce are equal to the additional revenue gained in production. This is identified by:

> Profit Maximization Point of Production
> $MC = MR$

Students often ask why the producer will not stop producing before the *MC* curve crosses the *MR* curve. The answer to this question is simply that his competitors will produce the extra amount that he didn't produce. If he stops production before others do, he will go out of business because the additional revenue his competitors gain will not be his.

Price	Quantity	MR	(−) MC	Difference(Gain)
5	1	5	3	2
5	2	5	2	3
5				
5				
5				
5				
5				
5				
5				
5				
5				

Why should this producer stop producing at quantity levels where *MC = MR?* Because beyond *MC = MR* is where *MC* is _____ than _____ _____, which means that if he produces beyond that point every unit he produces will cost more than he will earn.

Calculating Profit

Profit is calculated by subtracting average total cost (the average of his fixed and variable costs divided by the number of units produced) from total revenue. Total Revenue is $P \times Q$ (price × quantity). Profit is calculated at each level of production so that producers can see when and where profit erodes. The perfect competitor's profit will be the distance between the demand line and the bottom of the *ATC* curve.

Price ×	Quantity =	Total Revenue	− ATC =	Total Profit
5	1	5	15	−10
5	2	10	3	7
5	3	15	6	9
5	4	20	4	16
5	5	25	6	19
5	6	30	10	20
5	7	35	15	20
5	8	40		

Complete the table to show that beyond quantities of 8, Total Profit will become negative.

According to the $MC = MR$ rule for profit maximization, the producer should continue to produce up until unit # _____.

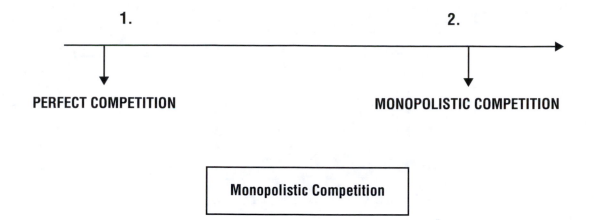

1.   **2.**

PERFECT COMPETITION   **MONOPOLISTIC COMPETITION**

Monopolistic Competition

In our market structure hierarchy, the Monopolistic Competitive Market is the second easiest market for producers to enter. It is called Monopolistic Competition because it borrows traits from both the monopolist's market and the perfect competitor's market.

■ Monopolistic: The monopolistically competitive structure is similar to the monopolistic structure in the following ways:

First. The monopolist (as we will see later) is a monopolist because he truly is the only seller of the good or service in question, or his market thinks he is the only viable supplier. In other words the demand that a monopolist sells to is very loyal. A monopolist could be selling a good or service that may have near substitutes, but if the demand for the monopolist's goods/services does not see the others as substitutes, then, at least to his buyers, he is the only supplier. The monopolistic competitor tries to create this same strict market loyalty.

Second. The monopolistic competitor faces a downward sloping demand curve. Some control over altering price is expressed by a downward sloping demand curve. A monopolist has the most vertical/downward sloping demand curve of any supplier.

■ Competition: The monopolistically competitive structure is similar to the perfectly competitive structure in the following ways:

First.   It is easy to enter. There are few if any regulatory hurdles to overcome and it is cheap. Fixed costs will be small.

Second.   The product sold is homogenous (_____).

Third.   There are many suppliers selling the same good/service.

Forth.   As single suppliers, each competitor has very little impact on the market supply.

The demand curve they each face is downward sloping but mostly horizontal.

List some Monopolistic Competitors:

_____

_____

How do you think a monopolistic competitor creates brand loyalty? (a downward sloping demand curve)

_____

_____

_____

A Monopolistic Competitor's Demand Curve.

Since the demand curve a monopolistic competitor faces is downward sloping, price will fall as quantity demanded increases. The table below shows you how quantity demanded increases as price falls. When price falls, the additional earnable revenue will

_____ as quantity _____.

Quantity	Price	Total Revenue	Marginal Revenue
1	8	8	8
2	7	14	6
3	6	18	4
4	5	20	2
5	4	20	0
6	3	18	−2
7	2	14	−4

A Monopolistic Competitor's Supply Curve.

Since a supply curve expresses what each unit costs to produce, and since the marginal cost tells a producer the per unit costs to produce, the Marginal Cost curve is the same as the _____ curve.

We already know how to calculate *MC* right? To calculate marginal cost we divide the change in total cost by the change in output. Since our output levels are changing in increments of one, we can divide our change in *TC* by one.

Quantity	TC	MC
1	5	5
2	9	4
3	12	3
4	14	2
5	17	3
6	21	4
7	26	5

Supply and Demand for the Monopolistic Competitor

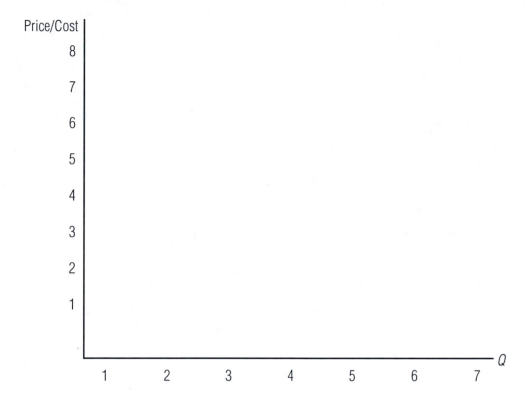

The fact that the demand curve is downward-sloping means the monopolistic competitor can change price up or down along the existing demand curve. If he increases price, he will _____ some quantity demanded. If he lowers price, he will _____ some quantity demanded.

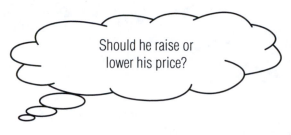

If he raises price from _____ to _____ , his total revenue will

_____ to _____ .

If he lowers price from _____ to _____ , his total revenue will

_____ to _____ .

> To increase total
> revenue he should lower
> his price.

To increase total _____ , he can lower price because the *MR* curve is

_____ _____ . Notice that even though the additional revenue

(____ ____) will _____ with each additional unit demanded, total revenue

will increase as more units are sold.

If he produces 1 unit his *TR* is _____ .

If he produces 2 units his *TR* is _____ .

If he produces 3 units his *TR* is _____ .

If he produces 4 units his *TR* is _____ .

If he produces 5 units his *TR* is _____ .

If he produces 6 units his *TR* is _____ .

If he produces 7 units his *TR* is _____ .

Beyond unit _____ his total revenue does not increase so he could produce that next unit, however, his *MC* will be greater than his *MR,* when he produces unit # _____.

So where should he stop producing and how much should he charge?

All producers in any market structure must answer the SAME two questions:

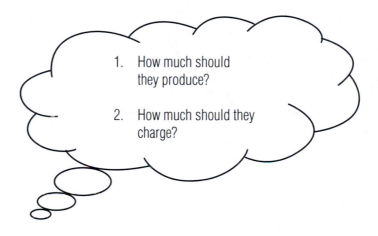

1. How much should they produce?

2. How much should they charge?

Question #1 relating to quantity produced is answered by where _____ = _____.

Quantity	MR	MC
1	8	5
2	6	4
3	4	3
4	2	2
5	0	3
6	−2	4
7	−4	5

Quantity	Price	Total Revenue	Marginal Revenue
1	8	8	8
2	7	14	6
3	6	18	4
4	5	20	2
5	4	20	0
6	3	18	−2
7	2	14	−4

In this case, the producer should produce up until quantity of _____, because beyond that point, *MC* will be greater than *MR*. If he stops producing before quantity of _____, he did not maximize his total revenue because total revenue for quantities less than _____ will be lower than what he could earn by producing _____.

Question #2 relating to price is a huge source of misunderstanding. Most people believe that producers can PUT price wherever they want. It cannot be true however because price is determined by where supply and demand meet. Since the demand curve is the consumers' expression of what they are willing and able to pay for various quantities, the producer cannot put price anywhere he wants unless he is in charge of crafting his consumers' demand curves, which he is not. Price is established by where supply and demand meet. Where they meet is determined by the slope of each curve and the slope of each curve is determined by the factors that create them.

To demonstrate how this is true, imagine a bowling alley.

Think of a bowling alley.

The wooden floor is shiny and very inviting.

The pins at the end of the lane are perfectly lined up.

The lane and the pins at the end represent supply.

The bowling ball represents demand.

Nothing happens to the pins until the ball makes contact with the pins.

The ball making contact with the pins represents demand making contact with supply.

Wherever they meet dictates the number of pins knocked over.

The number of pins falling is *price.*

So just like in a bowling alley, nothing happens until the ball knocks down the pins. In a supply and demand model, price will not exist until supply and demand meet.

A likely reason why people believe that suppliers are in charge of ***setting*** price is that, in a market, goods and services are labeled by a price. Think of these price tags as offers: suppliers are making Price ***Offers.*** People are therefore confusing the word offer with *Acceptance.* This is so because if people do not purchase the good or service for the asking price, then the asking price does not *become* the market price, and the good goes unsold.

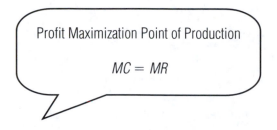

Profit Maximization Point of Production

$$MC = MR$$

The profit maximizing rule for the monopolistic competitor, however, is to produce output up to the point where *MR* crosses *MC,* just like the perfect competitor. This is where the additional revenue gained in production is _____ to the _____ _____ from having produced that extra unit. The connection between *MR* and *MC* establishes how much output the monopolistic competitor should produce. Price will be established by how much people are able and willing to spendfor that level of output.

Quantity	Price	MC	Marginal Revenue
1	8	5	8
2	7	4	6
3	6	3	4
4	5	2	2
5	4	3	0
6	3	4	−2
7	2	5	−4

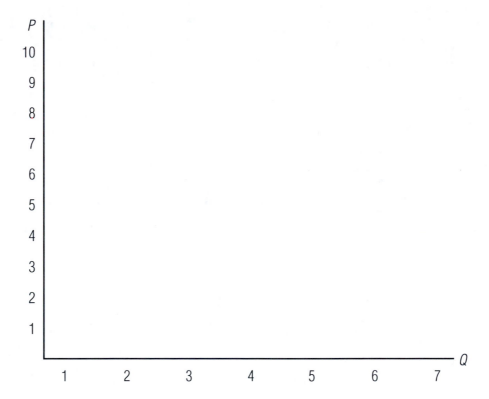

■ Re-plot your *MR* and Demand curves on the graph above.

■ Add to your graph an *MC* curve, by creating incremental costs that first decrease and then increase.

Find the intersection on your graph where *MC* = *MR*, and label it *PM* (profit maximization). This is the profit maximization output amount. From the connection between *MC* = *MR*, Draw dots up to the demand curve and label it *PM*[P] (profit maximization price level). To answer the question of what the producer will charge for his profit maximized output, the first question to answer is: How much does the demand curve say they are willing and able to pay for the amount he is producing?

Follow the level of output produced from where *MC* crosses *MR* straight up to the demand curve. That will be the level that the market says they are _____ and _____ to pay for the level of output being produced. The producer can charge what the market says they want to pay for that number of units. This role that demand plays in establishing price should clear up any notion that producers can and do charge whatever they want. What would happen if they tried to put price above the level noted as the profit maximization point on the demand curve? What would happen if they charged less than the price the market said they were willing and able to pay?

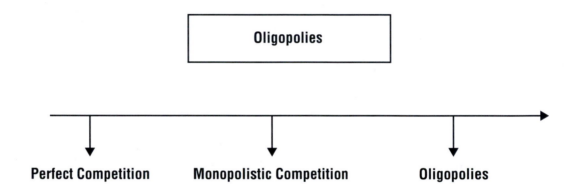

The third market structure is called an oligopoly. Oligopolists gain their unique identity by being one of few *powerful* suppliers in their market. There are generally five dominant companies that control roughly 60 percent of the market. The remaining 40 percent is shared amongst many small companies. The study of Oligopolies focuses on the severe competition that exists between the main five producers. Because it is so competitive, oligopolies try to escape price competition by using non-price competitive tools, namely advertising. The oligoplist tries to create strong brand loyalty with advertising as well as with other price discriminatory practices. To achieve loyalty, their advertising expenditures are high. The product or service they offer could be basically the same as what their competitors are selling and so the oligopolist usually tweaks or somehow distinguishes what he is selling with rewards, gifts, and bundled offers.

In addition to heavily advertising, oligopolies watch their competition very closely and try hard to gain accurate information on price, costs, new products, product lines, innovative changes, and any other factor that might cause them to lose their own power in the market. Due to the level of dependency between them, oligopolies are unsure of the demand curve they themselves face for the products they offer.

Market Demand

On the one hand, if their market sees their products as unique and irreplaceable (the way the market might see a monopolist product or service), then they will face a very _____ demand curve. On the other hand, if their market sees their product as easily replaced with a substitute, then they will face a demand curve that is highly horizontal (the way the market might see a monopolistic competitor's product or service). Because the oligopolist does not know for certain which demand curve he faces, he creates two separate curves.

Competitors Behavior

An oligopolist's competitor's behavior will also greatly affect which demand curve the given oligopolist faces. If airlines A raises the fare they charge to fly from LA to New York and all other leading carriers raise their price as well, then together they all face the same demand curve and it is very vertical (providing there are no substitutes outside of these carriers). If airline A lowers the fare they charge and all other leading carriers lower their price as well, then together they all face the same demand curve and it is very vertical.

Alternatively if one supplier should raise price by himself, then he will be acting alone and will loose a significant quantity demanded. If he should lower price and no other suppliers match his decreased price, then he stands to gain a significant quantity demand all to himself.

The "Kinked" Demand Curve Oligopolies faces

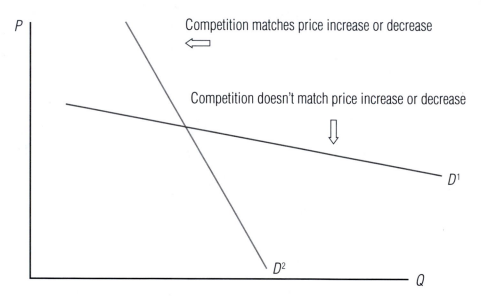

Mark the Price and Quantity Axes with numbers.

■   On the D^1 curve, how much demand is gained when price is lowered by one unit?

_____ How much demand is lost when price is raised by one unit?

_____.

■   On the D^2 curve, how much demand is gained when price is lowered by one unit?

_____ How much demand is lost when price is raised by one unit?

_____.

Conclusion:

1. Oligopolies have an inherent conflict of whether to raise price and increase *joint* profits, or lower price and increase *individual* company profits.

2. Oligopolies do not have perfect information about:

_____

_____   _____

In order to make up for this lack of accurate information, oligopolies create strategies to forecast their potential gains or losses by changing price (either through an increase or a decrease). The gain they earn may be dependent upon what their competitors do with their own price. This strategizing technique is called Game Strategy.

Game Strategy

Have you ever decided something was in your best interest regardless of what anyone else did? _____. If you answered yes, you have a Dominant strategy. A Dominant strategy exists when your choice of action is independent of another's behavior. If on the other hand your decision is contingent (dependent) on what the other person does, you have what is called a Nash equilibrium. Nash equilibriums are more common in the oligopoly structure because of the high level of interdependence between the players. Businesses use game strategy to determine whether they have a Dominant strategy or a Nash equilibrium by constructing tables of potential outcomes given by certain behaviors of their own and their competition. The question is generally whether they should or should not increase or decrease price. The question is important, because if they increase price and their competitors don't follow, what will happen to their market? Yet if they do increase price and the competition matches their increase, then suppliers gain because buyers have no other source that is selling for less.

Dominant Strategy

Competition breeds a loser and a winner. Competition happens when something is at stake or when the goal is something only one can achieve at the expense of others. If the object was not limited then competition would not be necessary because it would be available to anyone. When the object is not scarce, competition is not necessary. A Dominant strategy exists when a behavior is not limited by anything. If it is always better for you to tell the truth because your goal is integrity, then regardless of what is going on around you (incentive to lie exists), then you have a Dominant strategy to tell the truth.

A dominant strategy consists of the following:

- A best behavior

- A behavior that knows no limits

- A behavior that is not scarce

- A behavior that is best . . . always

- A behavior that is not scarce in action → Applies always

Nash Equilibrium

A Nash equilibrium exists when the goal is scarce but the players attempt to not compete. This eventually results in cooperation to not seek the scarce goal. Most Nash equilibriums result from one player's attempt to find a Dominant strategy but their mission is sabotaged by another's behavior. When your behavior is dependant on another's behavior, you do not have a Dominant strategy but rather a Nash equilibrium. A Nash equilibrium exists when one person's behavior IS contingent (dependant) on their opponents behavior.

Think of two products you consider being rivals. Enter the name of the first product in the top portion of each square. Under the dividing line, enter the name of the rival product.

Dominant Strategy

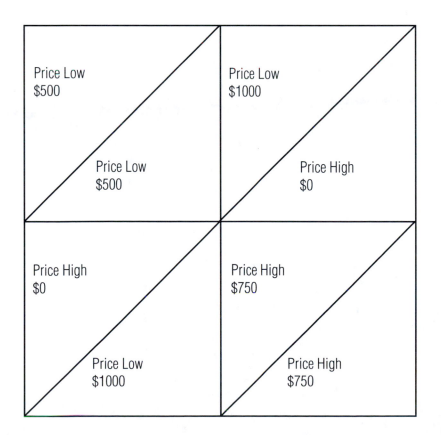

The dollar value expresses the potential gain to the company by pricing high or low.

Main Product Evaluation

Look at the gain to your main product when they price low. What are the potential gains as

listed? _____ or _____

Look at the gain to your main product when they price high. What are the potential gains as

listed? _____ or _____

Between the two choices of pricing high or low, which do you think the company should

choose? _____. Is this choice dependent upon what the rival does?

_____.

Conclusion

Your main company should price _____ and the decision is / is not contingent

on the rival's behavior. This means they have / do not have a dominant strategy.

Rival Company Evaluation

Look at the gain for your rival product when they price low. What are the potential gains as

listed? _____ or _____

Look at the gain for your rival product when they price high. What are the potential gains as

listed? _____ or _____

Between the two choices of pricing high or low, which do you think the company should

choose? _____. Is this choice dependent upon what your main company

does? _____

Conclusion

Your rival should price _____ and the decision is / is not contingent on the

other company's behavior. This means they have / do not have a dominant strategy.

Nash Equilibrium

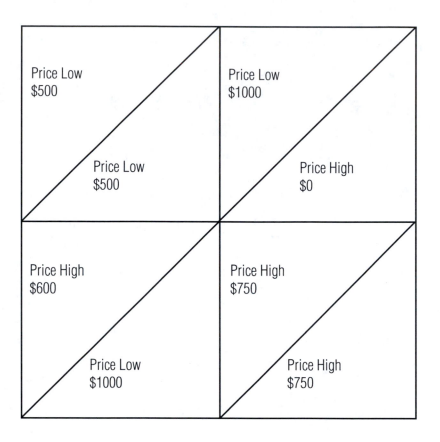

Write the name of your main product in the top portions of all squares, and write the rival in the bottom portion. The only difference between the Nash grid and the dominant strategy is that your main company stands to gain $600 (instead of zero) when it chooses to bid high. That pay-off amount is contingent on the rival bidding low.

Main Product Evaluation

Look at the gain to your main product when they price low. What are the potential gains as listed? _____ or _____

Look at the gain to your main product when they price high. What are the potential gains as listed? _____ or _____

Between the two choices of pricing high or low, which do you think the company should choose? _____. Is this choice dependent upon what the rival does? _____

Conclusion

Your main company should price _____ and the decision is / is not contingent on the other company's behavior. This means they have / do not have a dominant strategy.

Rival Company Evaluation

Look at the gain for your rival product when they price low. What are the potential gains as listed? _____ or _____

Look at the gain for your rival product when they price high. What are the potential gains as listed? _____ or _____

Between the two choices of pricing high or low, which do you think the company should choose? _____. Is this choice dependent upon what your main company does? _____

Conclusion

Your rival should price _____ and the decision is / is not contingent on the other company's behavior. This means they have / do not have a dominant strategy.

Think of a product that you know well by name: _____

In their market are there other well known brands? How many? _____

List the leading competitors:

_____

_____

When one of the suppliers raises price, what does your chosen producer do?

_____

_____

When one of the suppliers lowers price, what does your chosen producer do?

_____

_____

Does your producer heavily advertise? Where?

_____

_____

Look up the concentration ratio for your producer's industry? _____

A high concentration ratio means that the industry is concentrated with a select few powerful suppliers who control at least 60 percent of the market by themselves. The remaining 40 percent goes to the small, less well known suppliers.

Using the tables below, let's see what happens to an oligoplist when his competitors match his price changes and when they don't.

P	Q	TR	P	Q	TR
10	1				
9					
8					
7					
6					
5					
4					
3					
2					
1					

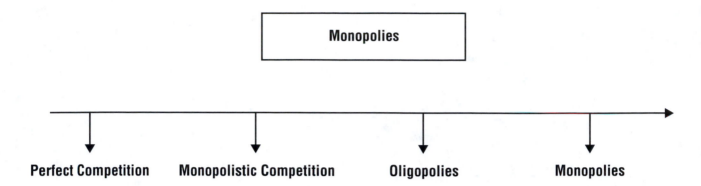

The final frontier of market structure is the famous monopoly. Mono means one, and so in this structure there is only one supplier. As a result, whatever the monopolist is producing, it must be so unique that there is no way to get the product elsewhere.

- Think of a company you believe fits inside of the monopoly market structure.

  _____

- Is it the only supplier of this product (are there any substitutes)? _____

- Are there high barriers to enter the market (cost, regulation, or patents/licenses)?

  _____

- Is your product a necessity? _____

■ Do many buyers buy the product when they do because they do not have time to find a near substitute? _____

If the answer to all of the above questions was yes, your supplier is probably a **monopolist.**

When all of the above questions are answered "yes," the demand curve the producer faces is a very vertical demand curve. A highly vertical demand curve means that most of the power is held by the producer and not the consumer. Power over what? Power over _____ much is _____ and power over how much is _____.

The Monopolist's Demand Curve

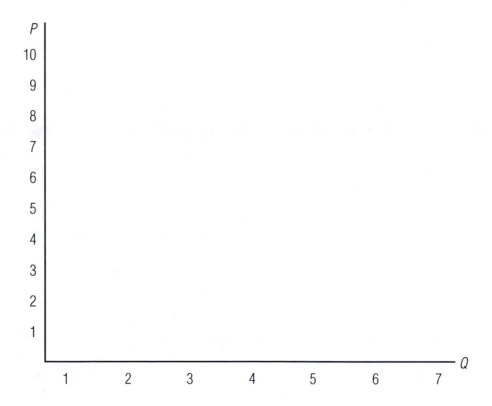

Quantity	Price	Total Revenue	Marginal Revenue
1	10	10	10
2			
3			
4			
5			
6			
7			

The fact that the demand curve is downward-sloping means that the monopolist has control over price. The monopolist can lower price or raise price. To increase total _____, the monopolist can lower price, because the *MR* curve is _____ _____. Notice that the additional revenue _____, will _____ with each additional unit demanded.

Compare this to the perfect competitor who faces a _____ _____ curve. The perfect competitor's demand curve is the same as his _____ _____ curve because he cannot increase _____ _____ by selling additional units.

The profit-maximizing rule for the monopolist like all other market structures is to produce output up to the point where *MR* crosses *MC*. This is where the additional revenue gained in production is _____ to the _____ _____ from having produced that extra unit. Where, however, should the monopolist put price?

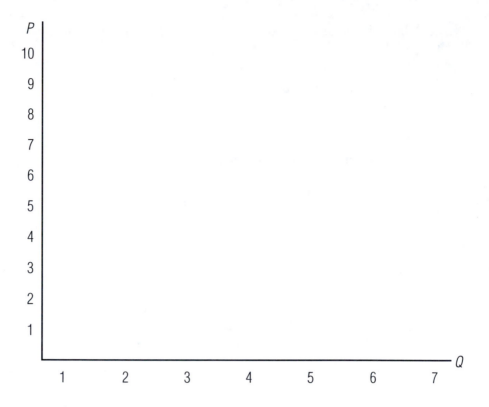

■ Re-plot your *MR* and Demand curves on the graph above.

■ We will add to your graph an *MC* curve by creating incremental costs that first decrease and then increase.

■ Next we will draw an average total cost curve. Your *MC* curve should intersect your *ATC* at your *ATC* curve's lowest point.

■ Find the intersection on your graph where *MC* = *MR*, and label it *PM* (profit maximization). From *PM*, draw dots up to the demand curve and label it PM^P (profit maximization price level).

Your monopolist will profit maximize by producing at output levels of _____.

Your monopolist will profit maximize by pricing above the intersection of *MC* = *MR* but along the demand curve.

The profits your monopolist earns are all price levels above the lowest point on the *ATC* curve. Price – *ATC*.

Observations: The monopolist could produce all the way up until: _____

The monopoly profits will be based on per unit profit since *MR* is decreasing with output.

Total profit is _____.

How Does a Monopolist Maintain His Monopoly?

A monopolist is able to become the sole supplier of a good or service in part due to the barriers to entry that exist. These barriers function similar to a shield that prevents other potential rivals from entering the market. Some barriers include:

a. Patents

_____

b. Franchises

_____

c. Control over key inputs

_____

d. Threat of, or actual lawsuit

_____

e. Acquisition

_____

f. Economies of scale

_____

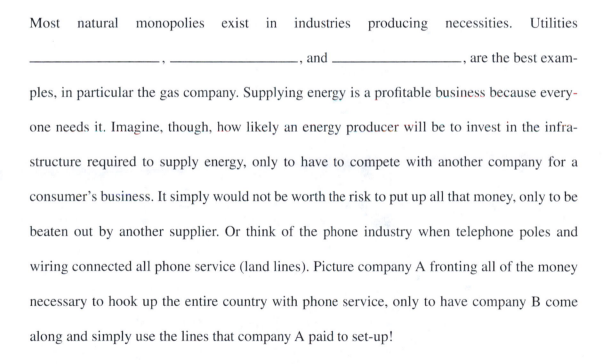

Natural Monopolies

In the natural monopolist market structure, the producer is a monopolist because no other producer can enter AND make a profit: there is only room for one producer. This results in only one company daring to enter and the market is served by only one producer, naturally. This market structure is very unusual because usually monopolists become monopolists from their entrepreneurial talents. Indeed, the natural monopolist may be producing something unique, but the dominant reason why they are the sole producer is because of the <u>enormous fixed costs that exist</u>.

Most natural monopolies exist in industries producing necessities. Utilities _____ , _____ , and _____ , are the best examples, in particular the gas company. Supplying energy is a profitable business because everyone needs it. Imagine, though, how likely an energy producer will be to invest in the infrastructure required to supply energy, only to have to compete with another company for a consumer's business. It simply would not be worth the risk to put up all that money, only to be beaten out by another supplier. Or think of the phone industry when telephone poles and wiring connected all phone service (land lines). Picture company A fronting all of the money necessary to hook up the entire country with phone service, only to have company B come along and simply use the lines that company A paid to set-up!

The Result?

Unless the company is assured of being the sole supplier, they will not bother to enter the market and consumers will have to go without.

How can these producers get this assurance? The government can limit the producers allowed

to produce by licensing requirements and regulation.

> Look up how it works . . .

In _____ county there are _____ producers allowed to pro-

duce or supply _____. The governing authority is _____.

New comers must _____ to be able to start supplying this market.

The Marginal Cost Curve and Supply

One supplier is all that is needed for efficiencies to occur. This is the case because the

_____ , or marginal costs associated with this product or service, actually de-

crease as additional output is produced. This happens because the high costs are the fixed

costs and all other costs are small in comparison (especially the marginal costs since they are

decreasing as output is created). In all other market structures however, marginal costs

_____ with additional output (and their fixed costs are not as high as the nat-

ural monopolist). In a competitive market structure, as new suppliers enter, costs fall.

BUT **Natural Monopolists** do **not need competition** to keep price from rising because their **marginal cost curve decreases** with additional output created. Yet, if competition is allowed, the natural monopolists *MC* curve will shift out and to the right and serve to raise their costs as well as the consumer price. (_____)

If the normal rule is to set price where demand exists at *MC* = *MR,* and *MC* shifts up as supply increases from competition in the market, then competition is not only unnecessary, but will cause the price consumers pay to increase.

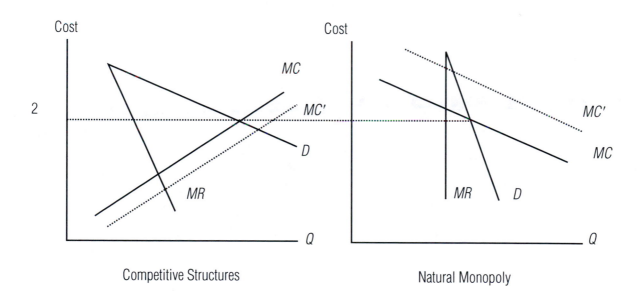

Competitive Structures   Natural Monopoly

If competition increases in the competitive model, price will fall. If competition increases in the natural monopoly, price will rise. Why? Remember that the marginal cost curve is the supply curve. When more producers exist, more output is created. If more output is created, then the supply curve pushes out and to the right. So if supply increases because more producers are supplying the market, then the *MC* curve will shift. In the case of the competitive structure, as more suppliers enter the market, the *MC* curve (the supply curve) will shift _____ and to the _____. In the case of the natural monopolist, the *MC* curve will shift _____ and to the _____ because it is downward sloping.

When the market is shared, profits erode as price falls. Price falls as many suppliers compete to capture the demand. This profit erosion then causes the one supplier to leave the market place because he cannot recoup the fixed costs that he had to pay to start the business in the first place.

- The Natural Monopolists' *MC* curve is _____ sloping.

- The Natural Monopolists' *ATC* curve is _____ sloping.

- The Natural Monopolists' Fixed costs are _____ than all other costs.

- As the Natural Monopolist produces more _____, marginal _____ decrease. This means that additional output gets cheaper and cheaper to produce.

The Natural Monopolists' Cost Curves

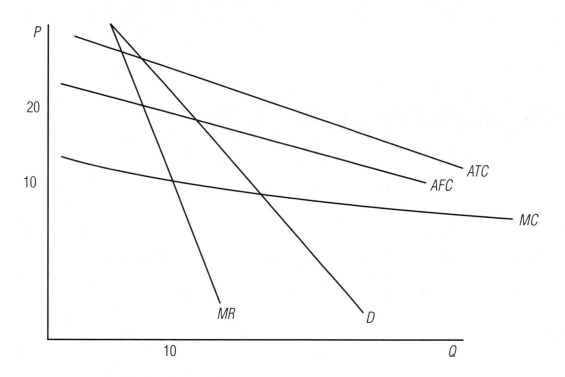

MARGINAL COST OUTPUT AND PRICING

Output

The natural monopolist should produce all output levels up until the point where *MC* crosses *MR*. This level will determine the output amount.

Pricing

The natural monopolist would like to put price where demand exists for that level of output where *MC* = *MR*. Is this the optimal price? No it is not the optimal price, because the natural monopolist is gaining from falling costs and not passing them on to the consumer. In other words, the natural monopolist experiences increased profit as he continues to produce and forces the consumer to pay a price that is higher than necessary because he is the only producer supplying the market with this product.

Can we solve this problem? Yes and No. In order to make sure that the benefits of a

_____ _____ are passed on to the consumer, the government

may _____ (require) a certain price, output, or profit level.

THREE DIFFERENT METHODS OF REGULATION

Price Regulation

If regulators forced the natural monopolist to produce where $MC = MR$, they could also re-

quire that the natural monopolist puts price where $MC = MR$. This is called price regulation.

A regulated price will be at the point where regulation would force the Natural Monopolist to

produce the level of output where $MC = MR = P$.

Mark your graph "*P*" where $MC = MR = P$. Label the price level Price regulation.

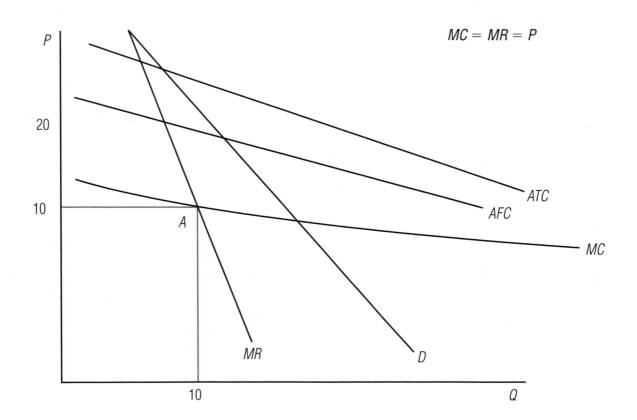

This is a great solution for the consumer because price will be extremely low. For the Natural Monopolist, however, this solution causes a loss on all units sold because *MC* continually decreases and is in fact less than *AFC* and *ATC*. Therefore if price is _____ than *ATC* and _____ _____ _____ , the natural monopolist's _____ will be higher than his _____ . A possible solution to these losses is to give the natural monopolist a subsidy.

The amount of the subsidy would be the difference between the regulated price and where *ATC* is for that level of output. Unfortunately, when price subsidies are offered according to costs, producers have been known to make their costs *seem* higher than they really are, in order to increase the amount of the subsidy. Padding _____ .

Profit Regulation

Profit regulation requires that the Natural Monopolist produce output where ATC meets with demand and put price at that same level. Find this level and mark it Profit regulation. This is a good solution for the consumer because the level of output produced will be a level greater than where *MC = MR*. It is also a good solution for the Natural Monopolist because they will not lose money on production, as price is equal to the average total cost of production.

Similar to price regulation, profit regulation may cause the natural monopolist to artificially increase average total cost in order to increase the _____ level.

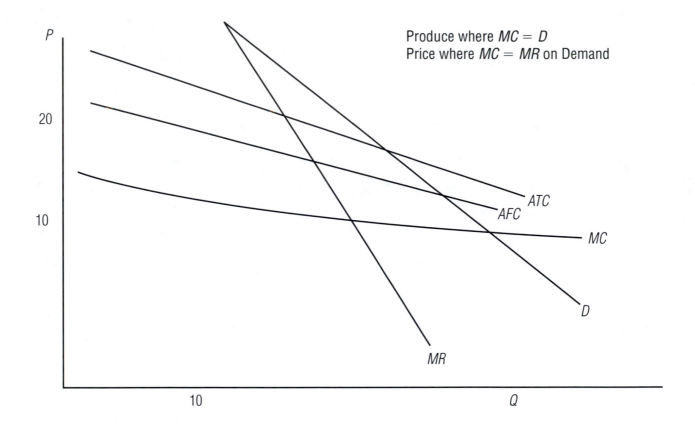

Output Regulation

A final way to regulate is through **Output Regulation**

Output regulation would allow the Natural Monopolist to price where $MC = MR$ on the demand curve, and produce where MC crosses demand. Find these two levels and label them "Output regulation." This solution is good for the consumer because the level of supply will be the level demanded. The natural monopolist is also satisfied in pricing where demand is above the intersection between MC and MR. But, like other forms of regulation, output regulation runs the risk of a loss in quality levels. The natural monopolist is being forced to produce output beyond his desired levels and in an attempt to meet this high level of output, he may neglect to pay attention to quality.

There are a handful of industries that have been regulated because they were natural monopolies. They were at times regulated and then deregulated, and in some cases, re-regulated. Using the Internet, look up the following industries to answer the questions.

Railroads

Why were they regulated?

_____

_____

_____

After they were regulated what happened? Good or Bad.

_____

_____

_____

Why were they deregulated?

_____

_____

_____

What is the industry like now?

_____

_____

_____

Airlines

Why were they regulated?

_____

_____

_____

After they were regulated what happened? Good or Bad.

_____

_____

_____

Why were they deregulated?

_____

_____

_____

What is the industry like now?

_____

_____

_____

Electricity

Why were they regulated?

_____

_____

_____

After they were regulated what happened? Good or Bad.

_____

_____

_____

Why were they deregulated?

_____

_____

_____

What is the industry like now?

_____

_____

_____

Cable TV

Why were they regulated?

_____

_____

_____

After they were regulated what happened? Good or Bad.

_____

_____

_____

Why were they deregulated?

_____

_____

_____

What is the industry like now?

_____

_____

_____

The Labor Market | CHAPTER 8

© iQoncept, 2010. Used under license from Shutterstock, Inc.

Why do people work?

1. _____

2. _____

3. _____

4. _____

The labor supply is defined as people who are _____ and

_____ to supply labor at specific amounts of time at alternative wages.

Why don't people work all of the time? What is the opportunity _____ of working?

1. _____

2. _____

3. _____

4. _____

Because there are choices there are costs to working. In order to compensate for those costs, employers must offer increasing wages to increase the quantity of labor supplied.

The labor supply curve is _____ sloping. This means that people will increase labor supplied as _____ increases. This is known as the income effect.

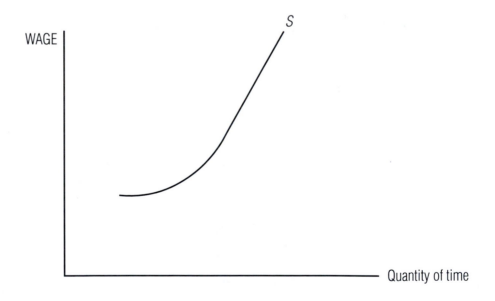

■   Ascribe numbers to both the quantity of time axis and the wage axis.

At wage rate = _____ the quantity of time worked is _____.

But, at wage rate = _____ the quantity of time worked is

_____ .

This is the law of _____. Workers will increase the supply of

_____ as _____ increases, holding all else

_____. This explains why the supply of labor curve is upward-sloping. There

is a _____ relationship between the quantity of labor and wage.

If that is the case, will the supply curve ever stop increasing? Yes, when the reasons for why peo-

ple work are no longer significant enough to _____ – _____

(opportunity cost) for what they have to give-up to work. In other words, people will reduce

the number of hours worked when what they give up is greater than income.

When the reasons to work no longer apply, the supply of labor curve may shift or even bend

backwards.

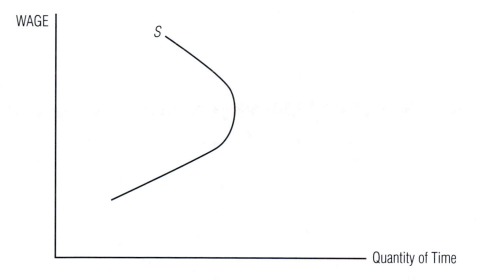

At wage rate of $5.00 a person works 10 hours.

At wage rate of $6.00 a person works 12 hours.

At wage rate of $8.00 a person works 12 hours.

At wage rate of $10.00 a person works 10 hours.

This is known as the substitution effect. Workers are able to substitute leisure for work, once their needs are met. Of course everyone has different needs/requirements for living, happiness, or satisfaction, and so individuals will have different supply of _____ curves. In part, this is why some people work more or _____ than others. In terms of economics, two things are happening when the curve bends backwards.

1. Dimishing Income Utility

    A worker's satisfaction or gain from earning more money and giving up leisure (other things in life) is less than it used to be: the opportunity cost of less leisure has increased. This is called diminishing marginal utility of _____. It means that the person gets less satisfaction from the additional income earned than from what they are giving up to earn the additional money. In other words, they can work less and gain more satisfaction in using their time in other ways.

2. Increasing Leisure Utility

    The curve will bend backwards when the person's satisfaction (utility) actually decreases from having to give up more and more time in order to work more hours.

    Does the supply of labor curve (what workers are willing and able to give up in order to work) establish what they earn?

                         Of Course Not!

In a market economy, price (in this case _____) is always established where

_____ and _____ meet.

The Demand for Labor

Who is in demand for labor? _____.

Why do they demand laborers? _____.

Laborers are a _____ cost. The only way to increase _____ is

to increase _____ costs.

Ok, so a producer will take on more variable costs in order to increase the output of what they

are selling, right? _____. Therefore the number of workers a producer will

demand is dependent upon how much demand there is for the product produced. This is called

derived demand. In other words, the extent to which an employer demands labor will be de-

pendent upon the product's sale price. So what establishes a product's sale price? From the

lessons learned in our study of market structure, price is established by the market structure.

Identify what power of price exists in the market structures below.

Market Structure	Power over Price
a. Perfect competition	None
b. Monopolistic competition	_____
c. Oligopoly	_____
d. Monopoly	_____

Depending upon what market structure the product being produced is in, producers will pro-

duce where $MC = MR$ and attempt to price where demand exists for that level of output.

Since we know that MC will rise as output increases due to diminishing marginal returns, the

producer must determine what level of output can be produced before diminishing returns

sets in.

Recall why diminishing returns occur:

_____

_____

The amount of labor a producer will hire will be equal to the amount they gain in hiring the worker. This level will be equal to the amount of output the worker is able to contribute times the price it can sell for. The Marginal Revenue Product is the additional revenue earned from a change in labor:

$$MRP = MPP \times \text{Price}$$

The *MRP* will decrease as more and more workers are added to the production process because of the law of _____ _____. This law says that total output will eventually stop increasing as more and more labor is added to fixed inputs.

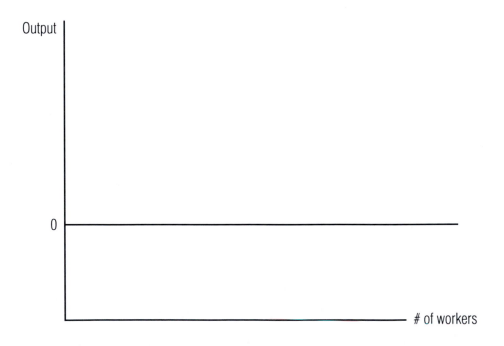

Observations

■ _____

■ _____

■ _____

A firm's labor demand will be given by the *MRP* of each worker. A firm will hire (demand labor) until the *MRP* curve intersects with the Supply of Labor curve.

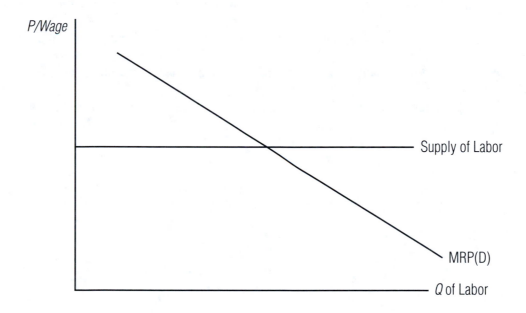

Assign numbers to both the *X* and *Y*-axes.

What is the wage rate? _____

Why is the *MRP* downward-sloping? _____

_____

Which way would the *MRP* curve shift if productivity (output/worker) increased?

_____

Observations:

■   _____

■   _____

■   _____

■   _____

The demand for labor has everything to do with what labor is producing. Labor is demanded because labor produces output. The rate of labor demanded will then connect with how much output they are producing. Remember, how much each worker contributes is called *MPP*. So we can expect that each workers contribution to total product (total output) will in part establish how many workers an employer (supplier) wants to hire (needs to hire). After we establish how many units any given worker produces we can construct a *MPP* curve. We can also construct a total product curve.

Let's create a Marginal Physical Product and Total Product Table.

Labor	Total Product	MPP
0	0	0
1	10	10
2	30	20
3	40	10
4	45	5
5	48	3
6	50	2
7	51	1
8	50	−1
9	45	−5
10	35	−10

As labor is added, total product begins to increase. Notice that *TP* increases at a decreasing rate and then *TP* begins to decrease at an increasing rate.

This is happening because of:

a.   The law of diminishing marginal returns, and

b.   adding only one variable input while holding all others constant.

A business owner should stop hiring additional workers (given the above information) after

worker # _____ because beyond that point total product turns negative.

Now we can create a price that these units are sold for. If they are sold for a flat amount then

we know that the demand curve for these products is flat. On the other hand, if the price falls

with additional units sold then we know that the demand curve is downward sloping. For sim-

plicity we will start with a product that is perfectly competitive. In other words, we will start

with a demand curve that is entirely flat. This means that buyers will buy one unit for some

amount and they will buy ten units for that same amount multiplied by ten. Price will not

change with an increase in quantity demanded because the demand curve is flat. Think back

about a flat demand curve for goods and services. What does a flat demand curve mean?

Labor	Total Product	*MPP*	Price	*MRP*
0	0	0	2	0
1	10	10	2	20
2	30	20	2	40
3	40	10	2	20
4	45	5	2	10
5	48	3	2	6
6	50	2	2	4
7	51	1	2	2
8	50	−1	2	−2
9	45	−5	2	−10
10	35	−10	2	−20

Definitions:

Labor: Variable Cost

Total Product: The total amount of output produced from all existing workers

MPP: The change in total output from each additional worker

Price: The price each unit sells for

MRP: The change in total revenue resulting from hiring one additional worker

MRP answers how much total revenue changes when one additional worker is hired.

Stop Hiring When . . . ??

We know that the employer will not hire workers when they are not contributing to an increase in revenue, but are there any other rules? Yes, we should also stop hiring workers when the cost of hiring them exceeds the *MRP* producers get from hiring them.

This should sound familiar. We should stop hiring after *MRP* < MC: or we should hire up until *MRP* = *MC*.

MC

So what is *MC*? *MC* is the cost producers must pay each worker. When all workers are paid the same, *MC* is constant. The supply of labor is flat because the workers working are all the same. They are perfectly competitive. They are all basic skill laborers. Nothing sets them apart. There are too many of them to count.

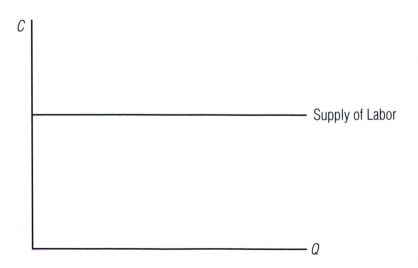

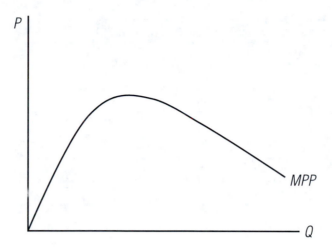

The demand for these workers will be in association with what they give the employer (the supplier: the producer). What each worker gives to the employer is assessed by his *MPP.*

Recap:

In this example, the labor supply is perfectly competitive: No one worker has more skill than another.

- The producer wants to hire more workers to increase output.
- Total output will increase at a decreasing rate as more workers are hired.

So we have two things going on at the same time:

- Workers are hired to increase output, but total output will stop increasing at a certain point.
- The producer must sell the output produced. Because the supply of labor is perfectly competitive the supply curve is flat. Also given that the skill of labor is perfectly competitive, usually the products being produced are also perfectly competitive. This means that the price the good is sold for will be fixed.

Labor	Total Product	MPP ×	Price =	MRP	Wage (MC)
0	0	0	2	0	6
1	10	10	2	20	6
2	30	20	2	40	6
3	40	10	2	20	6
4	45	5	2	10	6
5	48	3	2	6	6
6	50	2	2	4	6
7	51	1	2	2	6
8	50	-1	2	-2	6
9	45	-5	2	-10	6
10	35	-10	2	-20	6

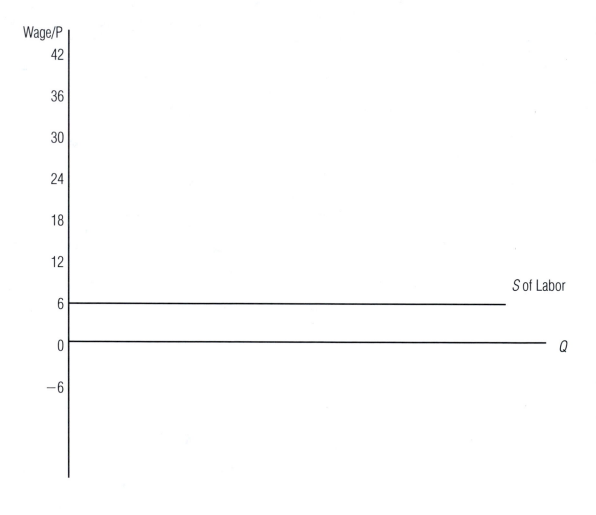

The Supply of Labor

The supply of labor will not always be perfectly competitive. In fact, the only time the supply of labor should be perfectly competitive is when all laborers are seen as the same. As soon as labor can be differentiated or distinguished, the supply of labor curve will have an upward sloping curve.

To use the same tools as established in market structure analysis determining price, the labor supply could be differentiated according to the level of skill that workers offer employers.

Recall the Factors of Supply

1. _____

2. _____

3. _____

4. _____

5. _____

6. _____

Now we can see how these factors create the amount of power that either workers or employers have over the market wage rate.

Perfectly Competitive Labor Supply

Workers with virtually no skills can offer employers manual labor. All non-skilled workers are _____ between one another. The employer does not care which of the _____ workers he hires. This means that there is nothing separating these workers from one another and as a result, the amount of power that each worker has over the market wage rate is zero. This is because as soon as one unskilled worker attempts to _____ for a higher wage, the employer will simply refuse to hire that worker and continue to use those workers that are offering services at the going rate. Therefore the unskilled labor market very closely resembles perfect competition. The supply curve for the perfectly competitive labor market will therefore be a _____ line.

Graph the labor supply curve in a perfectly competitive labor supply market

Wage

Q

Using the same logic, identify what might distinguish workers from one another in the remaining market structures below:

Monopolistic Competition

_____

_____

_____

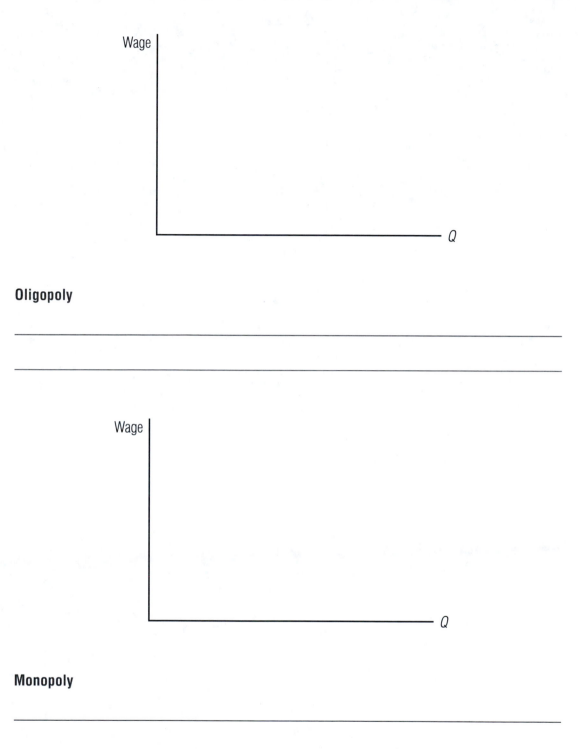

Oligopoly

_____

_____

Monopoly

_____

_____

The Demand and Supply of Labor and Wage

Now that we understand how both the demand for _____ and the

_____ of labor are established, choose any market structure for the demand

and supply of labor and graph where they intersect below. Identify which market structure

you used and explain the wage rate that is established.

What is the product or service being produced? _____

Supply of labor: Market structure → _____

Demand for labor: Market structure → _____

The supply of labor is _____ because it is a(n) _____ market structure.

The demand for labor is _____ because the product is sold in a(n) _____ market structure.

Wage is established by where the two markets meet given that the two market curves are established by their market structures.

Labor Unions

The purpose of labor unions is to cause equality between business owners (those in demand for labor) with workers (those in supply of labor). In terms of economics, this conversion is most often necessary when the labor supply is perfectly competitive. To convert a perfectly competitive labor market supply into a market structure that has power over _____ rates is what it is to create a labor union. Ordinarily, unions are found in industries where the supply of labor may potentially be abused in terms of wage rate, benefits, and job requirements. The potential for abuse of power from the employer to the employee is the result of the employer not being perfectly competitive while the employees are. Therefore there is an imbalance of power. In order to establish more equality, unions are essentially the conversion of a nearly perfectly competitive market into an artificial

_____ .

Just as a monopoly will lose power as soon as a substitute is available, unions generally

lose power as soon as substitute non-union labor supply becomes available.

Aka: _____

A union is only as successful as its ability to prevent _____

_____ .

How do unions work?

A union functions by bargaining with the employer regarding wages, _____ ,

and _____ . A producer will have _____ for union workers

because there are _____ substitutes available.

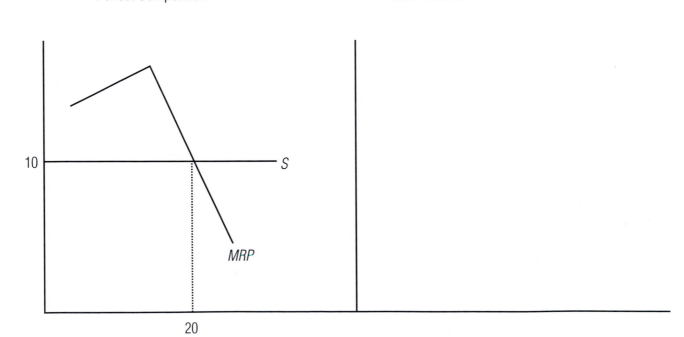

Perfect Competition   Labor Unions

Observations:

- The Perfectly Competitive labor supply is flat.

- The Labor Union Supply curve is upward sloping.

- In both markets the quantity of labor demanded is established by where *MRP* crosses the supply curve.

- In the perfectly competitive market, wage is established where *MRP* crosses Supply.

- In the Union market, wage is established where demand (*MRP*) crosses the upward sloping supply curve.

_____

_____

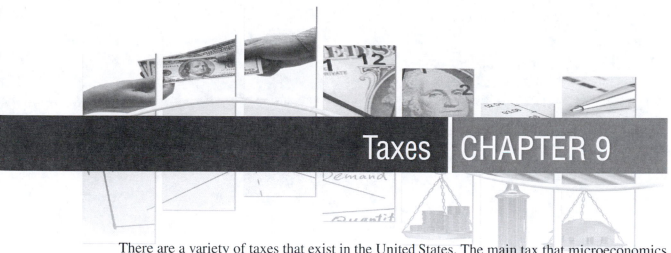

Taxes | CHAPTER 9

There are a variety of taxes that exist in the United States. The main tax that microeconomics is concerned with is the Federal Income Tax. The Federal Income Tax was first applied to a workers paycheck in _____. The original purpose of the income tax was:

_____

_____.

Over time, the system's purpose has grown to include redistribution of income from those that have more to those that have less.

Today, tax revenue serves two purposes.

1. _____

2. _____

Our goal is to understand the following:

■ If taxes are meant to pay for government spending, why does it seem as though our governments (State and Federal), are always in debt?

■ If taxes are also meant to cause some level of equality between income levels, why are people's income levels so different even after they have paid taxes?

Government Spending

The Federal Government depends on the Federal Income Tax (at a rate of _____

percent) to finance government expenditures. There are many reasons why this income might not

be enough.

A.   There is no cap on Federal Spending levels. _____

_____

B.   People can deduct certain expenses from their taxable income and pay less in taxes.

_____

Redistribution of Income (To Cause Equality)

If one major goal of the US Federal Income Tax system is to redistribute income from those

that have more to those that have less, we should first learn of how large the difference is be-

tween the rich and the poor. To make sense of how rich the rich are and how poor the poor are

in the US, we will divide the income of the United States into equal populations.

© Illin Sergey, 2010. Used under license from Shutterstock, Inc.

Some Facts:

The income of the US is called GDP. Look up the current income (real GDP) of the US.

_____ in Trillions of dollars: as of (date) _____ /_____/_____.

Ok Good, now we need the current population of the US. _____ as of

_____/_____/_____. If we divide the population into five equal groups, known as

quintiles, then we can see how much income (US GDP), an equal group of people earn.

Quintiles

Since both population and GDP figures change, the share of income any one group earns will

also change. For learning purposes we will use figures from 2009 to see how large income in-

equality is in the US, but keep in mind the new figures you have researched when looking at

the distribution. One quintile counts 20 percent of the population. If we calculate the popula-

tion using 2009 figures, we will use the figure of 300 million. Taking 300 million and divid-

ing by five (quintile), each of our groups will consist of sixty million people.

To use your current population amount:

- Multiply the population figure by .20 or 20 percent.

- In each of your five groups there are _____ million people.

If the distribution of the US GDP were exactly equal it would mean that all quintiles earn the same share of GDP. Take the current US GDP and divide by the total population to see how much income all _____ million people would receive.

The truth is, some people (many!!) do not earn even close to the amount you wrote above. No! The distribution of income (US GDP) more closely resembles the following:

US Distribution of Income 2009			
Income Quintile	**Income**	**Average**	**Share of US GDP**
Lowest 5th			
$_____ million	$0 – 18,000	$10,000	3.4%
Fourth 5th			
$_____ million	$18,000 – 34,000	$26,000	8.7%
Third 5th			
$_____ million	$34,000 – 54,000	$44,000	14.8%
Second 5th			
$_____ million	$54,000 – 87,000	$69,000	23.4%
Highest 5th			
$_____ million	$87,000 +	$147,000	49.8%

The Lorenz Curve

The Lorenz Curve graphically explains income distribution. Income equality will mean that the placement of the Lorenz curve is close to the income equality line. In other words, the closer the curve is to the absolute equality line, the smaller the difference between income levels (_____ _____).

Using the information from the column labeled "share of US GDP," plot the US Lorenz Curve.

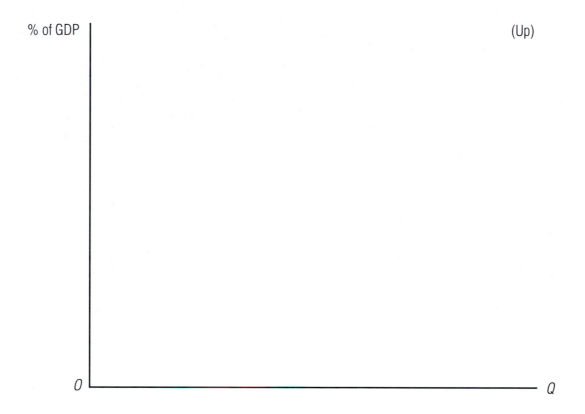

- Draw a 45° line starting at the zero mark. Your line should extend out and to the right toward the word "Up."

- Next mark your "x" axis population with your five quintiles beginning with the poorest level closest to the "0" mark.

- Next mark your "y" axis (percent of income) with the percentages of income distribution.

- Finally, connect the population points with the percent of income for each quintile and draw a connecting line (curve) between them.

What it means? The further the Lorenz curve is from the absolute equality line, the larger the income differences between population groups.

Conclusion: The US seems to be very unequal when it comes to how much people earn.

List the benefits and costs you can identify that accompany unequal income levels:

Cost   **Benefits**

_____   _____

_____   _____

_____   _____

_____   _____

As we have said, the Federal Income Tax has two separate purposes: to pay for government spending, and to try and equalize income levels. Whether or not taxation allows for either is a continually debated subject. However, as it is the system used, we should learn how it works.

The Federal Income Tax System

The Federal Government takes some amount of money from everyone's income check. The amount they take from people's checks represents roughly 45 percent of the government's total income. They will use this money to pay for government expenses and attempt to allocate some to those who do not earn enough to live.

The Federal Income Tax system attempts to accomplish both tasks by increasing the amount people pay as they earn more income. This is called a progressive tax: As you earn more, you pay more.

Income Breaks	Marginal Tax	Subtract to find the taxable income	% of Income taxed at this level	Incremental Tax
$0 – 7,000	10%	$7,000 − 0 = 7000	10% of 7,000	$700
$7,001 – 28,400	15%	$28,400 − 7,000 = 21,399	15% of 21,399	$3,209
$28,401 – 68,800	25%	$68,800 − 28,401 = 40,399	25% of 40,399	$10,099
$68,801 – 143,500	28%	$143,500 − 68,801 = 74,699	28% of 74,699	$20,916
$143,501 – 311,950	33%	$311,950 − 143,501 = 168,449	33% of 168,449	$55,588
$350,000 – 311,951	35%	$350,000 − 311,951 = 38,049	35% of 38,049	$13,317
			Total amount of tax to be paid	$103,829.00

This person is said to be paying a marginal tax of 35 percent. If he were really paying that amount; however, his tax bill would be $122,498.25, instead of $103,829.00. On average his tax is 30 percent (103,829 ÷ 349,995): taxes paid divided by total income.

In addition to the difference between the average and marginal tax levels, people are not taxed on their total income levels, but rather on their taxable income. Deductions, also called loopholes, change the amount of tax a person will pay, and will cause a person's taxable income to be different from their total income.

The law allows a person to deduct certain expenses from their taxable income, which makes the amount of tax on their income _____. Some of these deductions are allowed because of the hardship created in spending money on certain goods and services. For example, child-care, elderly care, home mortgage interest, and educational expenses are allowed.

These deductions serve to reduce the _____ between income levels, as well as change what is purchased as a result of the tax incentives in place. For example, people may not be as quick to purchase a house, were it not for the ability to deduct the interest payments on mortgage loans. A person calculates their taxable income by subtracting their deductions from their gross income. This creates two new problems that the tax system was created to fix.

- Vertical Inequities
- Horizontal Inequities

Vertical Inequities occur when a person who earns more income pays less in taxes.

Vertical Inequities

	Allison	Robert
Total Income	$90,000	$30,000
Deductions	− $70,000	− $5,000
Taxable Income	= $20,000	= $25,000
Tax	$7,000 @ 10% + 13,000 @ 15% = 2,650	$7,000 @ 10% + 18,000 @ 15% = 2,700
Nominal Tax (Taxes Paid Divided by the Taxable Income)	$2,650 / 20,000 = 13%	$2,700 / 25,000 = 10%
Effective Tax (Taxes Paid Divided by the Total Income)	$2,650 / 90,000 = 3%	$2,700 / 30,000 = 9%

Horizontal inequities describe those people who earn the same income but pay different taxes.

Horizontal Inequities

	Allison	Robert
Total Income	$90,000	$90,000
Deductions	$70,000	$20,000
Taxable Income	$20,000	$70,000
Tax	$7,000 @ 10% + 13,000 @ 15% = 2,650	$7,000 @ 10% + 28,400 @ 15% + 34,500 @ 25% = 13,610
Nominal Tax (Taxes Paid Divided by the Taxable Income)	$2,650 / 20,000 = 13%	$13,610/70,000 = 19.4%
Effective Tax (Taxes Paid Divided by the Total Income)	$2,650 / 90,000 = 3%	$13,610 / 90,000 = 15%

In-Kind Income and Welfare

In kind income and welfare are other methods the government uses to equalize income levels. Recall that the intention of the tax system was to cause greater _____ between _____ levels. The mission is to take from those who have a _____ level of _____ and give it to those who _____ _____.

In-Kind Income

When the good or service is given to the needy (rather than the income) it is called in-kind income. Think of goods and services that may be distributed to people who need it without any monetary payment for those goods and services.

_____

_____

These goods and services are consumed without any monetary exchange.

Welfare

When money is given instead of the good or service it is called Welfare. The governmental name given for welfare is TANF or Temporary Aid for Needy Families. All states have discretion over who qualifies as well as for how long they qualify to receive this money.

Look it up: What is the duration of time people may receive welfare payments in your state? _____ .

What income level constitutes the poverty line in your state?

$ _____

The Federal Government established what is called the poverty threshold in _____.
The poverty line is dependant upon the number of people in the family. A family of one, for
example, is considered impoverished by earning $ _____ per year. A family
of four meets the poverty level at $_____ .

The fundamental question of welfare is whether the government should guarantee the poverty
level of income. That is, should the government give a family the amount of the difference between what they earn on their own and the poverty level, to bring them up to the
$ _____ level?

If so, what problem may result from this "hand-out"? (Hint: Think about the incentive to work.)

_____

_____

_____

What other problems can you identify that may result from offering welfare in terms of:

■   States with different regulations

_____

■   Growth of GDP

_____

© Mavro Salvezzo, 2010. Used under license from Shutterstock, Inc.

OTHER TAXES:

Sales Tax:

Is it progressive or regressive?

_____

Who benefits from sales tax?

_____

Who is worse off because of sales tax?

_____

Who pays less sales tax, the rich or the poor? Why?

_____

Property Tax:

Is it progressive or regressive?

_____

Who benefits from property tax?

_____

Who is worse off because of property tax?

_____

Who pays less property tax, the rich or the poor? Why?

_____

Payroll Tax:

Is it progressive or regressive?

_____

Who benefits from payroll tax?

_____

Who is worse off because of payroll tax?

_____

Who pays less payroll tax, the rich or the poor? Why?

_____

Others:

Common Federal Taxes

_____

_____

_____

Common State Taxes

_____

_____

_____

Other Local Taxes

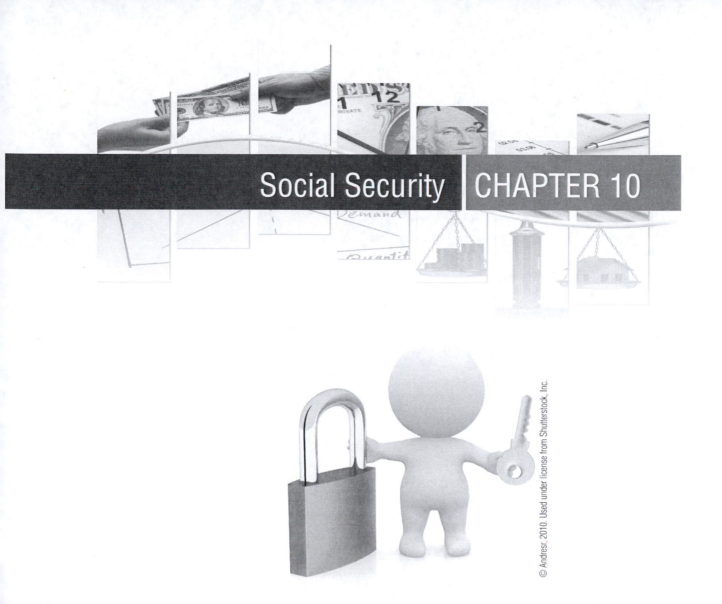

Social Security | CHAPTER 10

© Andresr. 2010. Used under license from Shutterstock, Inc.

Some Background

The Social Security system was created as a forced savings plan. Portions of workers' paychecks were withheld for the purpose of giving it back to them when they retired so they had some income on which to retire. It was created as a "pay-as-you-go" program. This meant that only the worker who paid into the system was able to draw out on their balance once they were retired. If, for example, the worker died before retirement, the money they paid-in would sit in reserve and be used in other ways. The retirement age at the time social security was created in 1935 was sixty-seven years old. At its inception, the number of people retiring as a ratio to the number of people paying into the system was one retiree to forty-three workers.

The Current Situation

As of 2003, that ratio flipped to three retirees to every one worker. Also, rather than simply paying the worker, the worker's family was allowed to draw on the workers' social security. Any excess money that would sometimes result from workers dying before they could collect social security was no longer there.

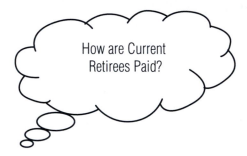

The money to pay retirees comes from the Social Security Trust Fund. This is where all prior years of collection have been deposited. The Trust Fund has historically been rich due to the fact that the population of workers has always been larger than the population of retirees. At times some of this money has been used to buy government securities.

Is this why there is doubt about whether everyone that has paid into social security will be able to collect? _____ !

During times of Federal government deficit spending, cash was needed. The Social Security Trust Fund had a surplus. In order to get the liquid cash to the governmental hands that needed it, Social Security gave up the cash it had on hand in exchange for government securities (bonds). In current times, this has caused the Social Security Trust Fund to have less cash than it would have otherwise.

Does it matter that the social security trust fund is cash poor?

The answer to this question is dependent upon the future of two key variables.

1. THE SIZE OF THE LABOR FORCE

The baby boomer generation (1946- 1964) is made up of 70 million people. As of 2031, the last of the baby boomer generation will be sixty-seven years old, the age of retirement. As of that date, these retirees will be seeking social security payments. The current US population is ____ million. The current labor force is made up of ____ million workers. So in order to pay these retirees the labor force must _____ at a faster _____ than the rate of the retiring _____. The question that needs answering is where will the growth in the labor force come from?

Your thoughts:

_____

_____

_____

_____

2. THE DEMAND FOR GOVERNMENT SECURITIES

The Social Security Trust Fund holds government securities. When retirees demand their social security payments the money traditionally comes from the funds available. When the funds are not available, the Trust Fund must sell off the securities it holds to pay those retiring the cash they demand. As long as the trust fund can find buyers of these securities, there is no problem. Therefore, unless people stop buying government _____, the social security administration will be able to pay retirees their _____.

Ok, so what might cause the demand for securities to shrink?

Any change in the factors of _____ can cause the demand for securities to shift. Recall the factors of demand. (Hint: There are five.)

1. _____

2. _____

3. _____

4. _____

5. _____

Of these factors, expectations may be the most important issue when it comes to the securities market. The central component to giving up cash today is the interest earnable in the future. If the earnable interest is too low, then people will demand other assets and not government securities.

Ok, but what might cause the earnable _____ _____ to decline? To answer this question, you must know which curve creates the current rate of interest. The _____ for bonds and where it intersects with the supply of bonds (where the government is _____ and _____ to supply bonds) is what establishes the current interest rate on securities. So a loss in demand for securities will cause the earnable interest in securities to decline, which will cause a second decline in demand, which will cause a larger decline in earnable _____, and the scenario will simply perpetuate.

Conclusion

As long as the labor force can replace itself, or at least grow at a rate that is

_____ than the _____ of growth of the _____,

AND as long as the demand for _____ stays strong, social security will

continue to be funded.

Notes:

_____

_____

_____

_____

Financial Markets | CHAPTER 11

© donatas 1205, 2010. Used under license from Shutterstock, Inc.

All markets have products. What is the product of a financial market? _____.

The reason _____ is a product for sale is because some have it and some do not. In other words, money is a _____ resource.

The supply of money represents the supply of loanable funds.

How do those that need money (_____) locate those that are offering

(_____) it?

_____

_____

_____

Financial Intermediaries: Stocks

What is stock? If you could ask a friend for some money and promise to give him a portion of the profits you make from borrowing his money once you produce _____, then your friend has a stake in how well your company performs. This stake in performance is stock. He owns a portion of whatever you create with the money you borrowed from him. Stocks vary by the type of company asking for your money:

A. Corporate Stock: If a corporation is asking for your money, and they fail to perform (pay you), they owe you nothing. The reason you would ever agree to give such a corporation any of your money is because they will pay you more (dividends) than other companies if they succeed.

B. Partnership: If you buy stock in a partnership, the owners of the company are liable to the success of the company together, the way partners are.

C. Proprietorship: Proprietorships are companies owned by single individuals. You can buy stock directly from the owner, but the stock is not publicly traded.

What are the payoff amounts dependent upon? Payoff is dependent upon how well the company does. The amount you receive is called a dividend. Some stocks do not offer dividends and instead promise to take your investment and carry it into the future for investment. This is called retained _____. It is the amount shareholders should be given but is instead kept by the company to increase investment and therefore future _____. When this investment then causes an increase in profit for the company, it is called a capital gain.

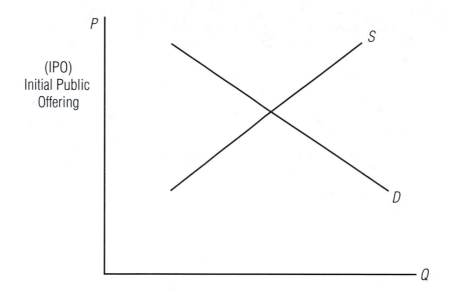

The Set Up

■ Company "A" needs money.

■ Company "A" lists stock for purchase in an initial public offering on the stock exchange.

■ Price is established based on where demand meets this supply (IPO).

What will happen to demand if expectations of the success of the stock diminish?

_____

What will happen to price if the supply of stock increases?

_____

Find the price and quantity combinations where $S = D$.

Price = _____ Quantity = _____

Calculating the Gains of Stock Ownership

How does a person know what they stand to gain in stock ownership? That profit is expressed in terms of price per earnings ratio. The price per earnings ratio is the price of the stock share divided by the earnings each share yields.

A. Price per Earnings Ratio: Share Price ÷ Earnings per Share

For example if the share price is $18.00 and the earnings per share is 79 cents, then The price per earnings ratio is 22.8, or $18.00 ÷ .79 = 22.8. This is the value per share that you stand to gain. To express the true gain however, the opportunity cost of being without the money you invested must be subtracted from the gain. This is called the rate of return on the dollar and is calculated by dividing the price per earnings ratio into one.

B. Rate of Return on the Dollar: 1 ÷ Price per Earnings Ratio

The one represents the per dollar amount. To calculate the rate of return (what your dollar today earns you when you give it up), 1 ÷ 22.8 = 4.4%

What does this mean? It means that if you give up your dollar today, it will yield you 4.4% tomorrow.

This number however does not factor in any potential risk of company failure. To include the risk factor, you have to subtract the chance of company failure from the expected value. If the company has a 25 percent chance of failure, that amount must be subtracted from potential earnings.

C. Earning Potential minus Risk Factor:

1 − Risk Factor ÷ Earnings per Share

Earning potential including the risk factor (1 − .25) × .79 = .59

D. Real Expected Rate of Return:

Earning Potential with the Risk Factor ÷ Price per Share

Therefore, a person who invests money in this stock market must understand that their expected rate of return is not 4.4% but rather:

$$.59/18.00 = 3.2\%$$

This amount includes the risk factor of failure. In other words, the true _____

cost of giving up today's dollar.

This might mean that it is better to have money today for your own consumption, than give it to a company in the form of stock.

How will we know?

By what is called the **Time Value of Money.**

© Adem Demir, 2010. Used under license from Shutterstock, Inc.

The Time Value of Money

How do we assess the value of money? It is better to have _____ today, rather

than later. However, if you choose not to have your money today, then you must be compensated for the opportunity cost of not having it **NOW.**

To determine if it is worth it to give up your cash today for the sake of more tomorrow, we need to understand what the opportunity cost of not having money today is: It is evaluated in terms of the _____ rate.

The Present Value of Money

Interest rate determines what today's dollar will be worth _____. Trying to understand what the present value of money is according to the potential future gain of that money is answered by the present value of money. The present value of today's dollar is equal to its future value divided by one plus the earnable interest rate.

$$PV = FV \div (1 + \%)^n$$

Where: PV = Present Value
FV = Future Value
$\%$ = Interest Rate
n = represents the number of periods

How much money do you need to start with?

Apply the formula: In order to have $10,000 in three years time, what amount of money must you save and at what rate of interest?

$$PV = \$10,000/(1 + .045)^3$$

Year one: $10,000/1.045 = $9569.37 (1st period)

Year two: $9569.37/1.045 = $9157.29 (2nd period)

Year three: $9157.29/1.045 = $8762.97 (3rd period)

This means that in order to reach $10,000 in three years at an interest rate of 4.5 percent, a person must start with $8,762.97.

Present value is also used to decide between two methods of payment.

Is it better to receive $10,000 now, or receive $10,000 in three years at a rate of interest of 4.5 percent?

$$\text{Year One: } \$10,000 \times .045 = \$10,450.00$$

$$\text{Year Two: } \$10,450.00 \times .045 = \$10,920.25$$

$$\text{Year Three: } \$10,920.25 \times .045 = \$11,411.66$$

This means that waiting to receive $10,000 is acceptable when the cost of waiting is less than $1,411.66, which is the amount earned from having waited.

Present Value vs. Future Value

Is it better to have $15,000 today or $18,000 in four years at 4 percent?

Calculate the present value of a future payment given the following:

Step 1: $18,000 × (1.04) = _____ in the first year

Step 2: $18,720 × (1.04) = _____ in the second year

Step 3: $19,468 × (1.04) = _____ in the third year

Step 4: $20,247 × (1.04) = _____ in the fourth year

Present Value: $15,000

Future Value: $21,057

The difference between $15,000 and $21,057 is $6,057. This amount represents the opportunity cost of waiting for $15,000 for four years.

_____

_____

_____

The Farm Problem | CHAPTER 12

When you think about food (not the boxed and processed kind, but the kind that grows in the ground and on trees), do you think of a highly profitable industry? _____

Why or why not?

_____

_____

From what you have learned, what makes an industry profitable?

_____

_____

Ok, so farming is probably not very profitable given what we have learned about in our market structure studies. But was it ever profitable? _____ it was before the key elements that caused supply to increase at a rate that was faster than demand to consume.

Prior to 1919 the price that agricultural; i.e., _____ goods sold for was historically high.

Why was the price so high?

At the time, the ratio of farm workers to machines was four to one. This caused supply to not

_____ even when _____ was strong. In other words, supply

was low enough to keep the price from falling away from the current level of demand. When

global demand increased in 1919 (WWI), supply could not keep up and as a result, price re-

mained _____.

Draw a Demand curve: label it *D*.

Draw a Supply curve: label it *S*.

Find the equilibrium price and quantity levels, and ascribe numbers to those levels.

Draw a second Demand curve: Label it *D increase*.

What happened to price when demand increased? _____

What happened to quantity supplied when demand increased? _____

These were the conditions by which the agricultural industry was solvent before the 1st Farm

Depression of 1920-1940.

What Happened?

In 1920 there was a decrease in demand because of new international trade restrictions. Also during that same time, there were large gains in production due to an increase in efficiencies. By 1921, farming prices fell by _____ percent compared to their 1910 price levels. By 1932, these same prices fell by _____ percent of the 1914 prices.

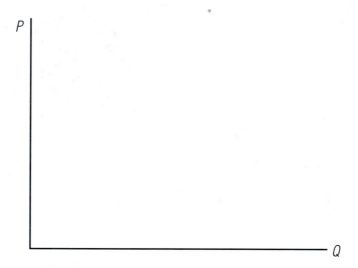

Using the information above, graph what happened during the first farm depression.

The 2nd Farm Depression (1980–1986) created a loss in income for farmers that fell below the loss of 1932–1933. This time the reason was largely due to an increase in the production costs due to an increase in fuel costs by _____ percent. Interest rates were also significantly high at _____ percent, which then caused a decrease in land values. To a farmer, a decrease in land value is equivalent to _____.

At the same time as costs were increasing, the productivity level of output was increasing because of the productive machinery (the ratio of machines to farmers flipped to one worker to four machines). Another ingredient that increased output was highly productive fertilizer.

Overall Issues Today

Output has increased by 70 percent as compared to the _____ levels, while labor has decreased by _____. Why? What has happened is that farming has become too _____ over the years because of the following factors:

- High yield seeds

- Advanced machines

- More productive fertilizer

- An increase in animal breeding

- Computer management systems

- Improved and more weather resilient plants

- More efficient use of land through learned crop rotation processes

A Continuous Surplus

Is a surplus bad? Not usually, but in the case of agricultural goods, people cannot consume more food simply because price is falling. But a falling price is good! Not if the falling price is your income.

Recap:

We have too much food because the industry has become too _____. As a result the _____ curve keeps shifting _____ and to the _____ . This causes the price of food to _____. Usually when the price of anything falls, quantity demanded increases. But this does not happen in the case of food products because a sale on food (lower _____) does not get people to demand more _____.

Why not? Recall price elasticity:

_____

_____

Because of this the demand curve for food looks like this:

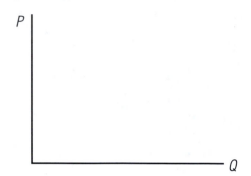

This means that even though price is falling, _____ _____

does not increase in-kind. The demand curve stays where it is as supply keeps

_____ and farmers make less and less income.

Solutions to the Farm Problem Since 1919

1.   **Price Floors – offer an artificially high price:**

New Problem: this entices new entrants that further _____ supply. The new

problem becomes: How to get rid of surplus?

2. Set asides:

_____

Idle land: 1995–50 million acres idle; 1.6 million cows slaughtered.

New Problem:

_____

3. Marketing Orders:

Farmers collectively destroy the supply to keep prices artificially high.

New Problem:

Serves as an enticement to enter because profits exist. This further increases supply.

4. Import Quotas:

Restrict the level of imports and _____ taxes on imports. This is an attempt

by the government to try and inflate demand for domestic products.

New Problem:

_____

5. Government Stockpiles:

Through the CCC (Credit Commodity Corporation), who is a buyer of last resort, a farmer can sell his supply to the CCC if the market price is below the CCC price. If the market price is above the CCC rate, the farmer sells its supply on the market and repays the CCC for previous loan amounts and keeps any difference.

New Problem:

_____

6. Counter Cyclical Payments:

Similar to a simple direct income support program where target prices are identified by Congress—just like a price floor. If the market price falls below the target, the government makes up the difference between the market price and the target price.

New Problem:

_____

Overall:

Operating primarily through the 2002 Farm Act, the US Department of Agriculture aids farmers in a variety of ways. Some versions of aid are connected to productivity; some versions are connected to a fixed sum.

_____

_____

_____

_____

_____

_____

_____

_____

_____

_____

_____

Enviromental Protection | CHAPTER 13

How does economics answer the problem of pollution? First and foremost, economic theory holds that it is impossible to entirely be rid of pollution. Why? Because everything is _____. In the case of pollution, the very existence of only clean/pure anything is impossible because everything is scarce. Therefore, economists look to see what benefits and costs come with pollution. There are obviously many environmental dangers other than pollution but the economic treatment of all environmental concerns can be understood in the same way economics handles pollution.

How does Economics Solve for Pollution?

So far all questions have been answered with our equation by setting the marginal cost equal to the marginal benefit: $MR = MC$. In the case of pollution, MC represents all of the incremental costs that come from pollution. MR is translated into MB, which stands for marginal benefit. The marginal benefit represents the incremental gains that come from diminishing pollution. The economic answer to solving for pollution is to set the MC of controlling pollution equal to the MB of controlling pollution: $MC = MB$.

Why Does Pollution Occur?

Polluting is cheaper than not polluting for the polluter, but for society and the environment, pollution is very expensive. The reason it is cheaper for producers to pollute is because being careful when it does not benefit them directly is equivalent to adding a new cost to their production costs. As soon as producers are forced to watch emission levels or account for where they got the water to cool their towers and how or where they disposed of said water, their costs increase. Obviously there are far greater and more damaging behaviors that occur in a production process, but the rationale for how pollution is evaluated is the same.

As long as producers do not directly reap the benefits of a "clean" operation, they will not spend any time or money on careful production processes. It is cheaper to _____ and have others bear the cost for that pollution than it is for producers to include those costs in their costs of _____ .

What Is the Desirable Level of Pollution?

Given that producers will not reduce their level of pollution voluntarily, how much abatement (regulation) is desirable or more importantly, worthwhile? The socially optimal level is where the *MB* (of abatement) is set equal to the *MC* (of abatement).

What does this mean?

Essentially it means, "do not spend $100,000.00 to save ONE fish." It means that the benefits (saving the fish) should equal the cost of having saved it (no fish to have).

How Does Regulation Deter Pollution?

Pollution abatement is accomplished by altering market incentives. When producers do not include pollution costs in their cost of production, they will produce more polluting output as they produce more output. The producer will be able to continue to produce at a lower cost as a result of not including all of the true costs of the resources he is using for free, not to mention all of the unknown costs. The result of not including all costs creates a false supply curve, because the supply curve is a product of the costs of production. As a result, the market price for which the product sells will be less than it should be. This is an economic danger because price is meant to represent the true cost and value of the good or service. If all costs are not included, then the final market price will not be representative of the true value and cost of what is being sold. Therefore, in order to cause the real cost of production to be included in the producer's price, the government will regulate the producer for polluting. This does not mean that the producer will stop polluting but rather that he will have to pay for polluting. The goal of pollution abatement becomes that of "hitting them where it hurts," or making polluters pay for having polluted. This serves as an incentive to reduce the amount of pollution emitted because they are now forced to pay for doing so. Additionally, because their costs of production rise, they will charge more for the final product sold to the end user. As the price increases, the quantity demanded will decrease. In this manner, the true economic cost and benefit of the product is revealed.

The mechanisms used to achieve this result (taking the social [external] costs and making them private) include:

Fees

_____

Technology

_____

Recycling Mandate

_____

User Fees

_____

Taxes

_____

Marketable Permits to Pollute

_____

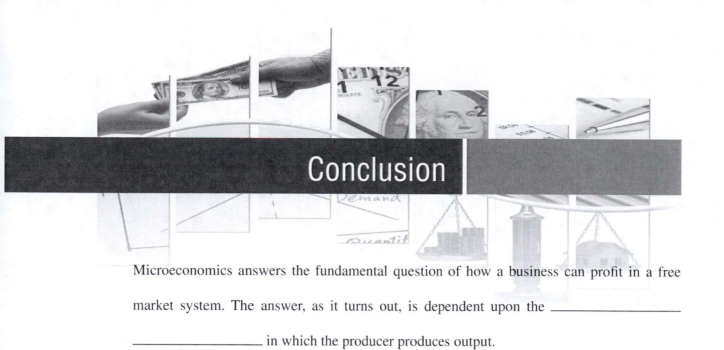

Conclusion

Microeconomics answers the fundamental question of how a business can profit in a free market system. The answer, as it turns out, is dependent upon the _____ _____ in which the producer produces output.

This basically means that some of the profitability prospects are under the control of the producer, while other variables are not. No matter the goal of the producer, there is one consistent rule that always holds true:

All Decisions Should Occur When

____ ____ = ____ ____ .

Ok great, what else have we said?

Well, as it turns out the *MC* = *MR* rule crosses over to all other microeconomic concerns as well. Really? Yes. Starting backwards:

Environmental Protection

Control pollution up until the benefits of controlling it match the costs of controlling.

MC of Pollution Control = MR (MB) of Pollution Control

The Farming Problem:

The *MC* of subsidies must be set equal to the marginal revenue of keeping the industry alive in this country. As soon as the subsidy amount is greater than the cost of not producing food domestically, subsidizing the industry is a mistake.

$$MC \text{ (of the subsidy)} = MR \text{ of subsidizing}$$

Financial Markets:

This is easy: If the long term payoff (dividends + the cost of not having your money available to spend today) is less than the benefit of having the money today, the opportunity cost of giving up your money today is too high. *MC* > *MR*.

$$MC \text{ of not having money today} = MR \text{ of having money tomorrow}$$

Social Security:

As long as the marginal cost of holding government securities is equal to the marginal revenue of carrying government debt, social security will remain solvent.

$$MC \text{ of Bond Creation} = MR \text{ of Bond Sales}$$

Taxes:

The tax system fails to cause equality because the marginal revenue of escaping taxes is greater than the marginal costs of paying taxes equally: a systems error.

$$MC \text{ of Paying Taxes} = MR \text{ of Taxes Paid}$$

The Labor Market:

Wage (marginal cost) should be equal to the marginal revenue gained in the sale of the output labor produces.

Market Structure:

All market structures profit where they produce up until quantity levels of $MC = MR$.

Growth

Today's expenses could sabotage tomorrow's growth prospects. Do not choose that behavior that puts the incremental costs above the incremental benefits of having made that choice: opportunity cost.

$$MC \text{ of not spending today} = MR \text{ of Savings Tomorrow}$$

Optimality

There is a cost to every choice. As long as the next choice and the benefit it yields are greater than or equal to the cost of the choice, the optimal condition exists.

$$MC \text{ of this Choice} = MR \text{ of this Choice}$$

Economic Systems

Of the economic choices that must be made, the choice of the economic system can make or break the economic outcome. We cannot rationally choose a system that decides what will be made, how it will be made, and who will receive the profits from having made it, and then wish the outcome to be different from the outcome the system decides. If everything is scarce then we are sure that when we pick what we pick, we are giving something up in return. It is up to us to decide if what we have picked, $MR;$ is equal to the costs of picking what we picked, MC.